The Catholic Mystery

John H. Armstrong

HARVEST HOUSE PUBLISHERS
Eugene, Oregon 97402

Unless otherwise indicated, Scripture quotations are taken from the Holy Bible, New International Version®. Copyright © 1973, 1978, 1984 by the International Bible Society. Used by permission of Zondervan Publishing House. The "NIV" and "New International Version" trademarks are registered in the United States Patent and Trademark Office by International Bible Society.

Verses marked NASB are taken from the New American Standard Bible, © 1960, 1962, 1963, 1968, 1971, 1972, 1973, 1975, 1977 by The Lockman Foundation. Used by permission.

Verses marked KJV are taken from the King James Version of the Bible.

Cover by Terry Dugan Design, Bloomington, Minnesota

THE CATHOLIC MYSTERY

Published by Harvest House Publishers
Eugene, Oregon 97402

Library of Congress Cataloging-in-Publication Data

Armstrong, John H. (John Harper), 1949–
The Catholic mystery / John Armstrong.
p. cm.
ISBN 0-7369-0103-5
1. Evangelicalism—Relations—Catholic Church. 2. Catholic Church—Relations—Evangelicalism. 3. Catholic Church—Doctrines. I. Title.
BR1641.C37A75 1999
282—dc21 99-22974
CIP

Printed in the United States.

99 00 01 02 03 04 05 / BP / 10 9 8 7 6 5 4 3 2 1

For the new reformation that is
desperately needed in our time.

And for my firstborn, Matthew John Armstrong,
who has lived in a manner that honors the name
given by his parents, "gift of the Lord."

Matt, you not only bring great joy to your father
and mother as you seek after the kingdom of God
with all your heart, mind, soul, and strength, but
your love for those who need Him far exceeds
anything I could have ever asked or hoped for.
You live as a reformer who courageously
pursues God's call upon your life.

Acknowledgments

I am in continual debt to the board members of Reformation & Revival Ministries, Inc., who give time, friendship, and support in order that I might labor for the reformation of the church in this generation.

Thanks to Michael Valentino, a brother who genuinely understands the Catholic mystery, thanks God for what he learned through it, and is now willing to follow the Scripture when and where God leads. Your input made this a better book.

Harvest House has again shown me what a good relationship with people can do for an author and his publisher. A special thanks is in order for Steve Miller, my editor. You have helped make this book better by your significant and needed input. Steve, your daily faithfulness to use your gifts through your own weakness and solid joy inspires me to be even more faithful. And thanks to Bob Hawkins, Jr., who takes the time to hear me, support me, and trust me.

A debt of deepest gratitude is always in order to Anita, my wife of nearly 29 wonderful years. You protect me as a man, serve me as a writer, and encourage me as a person. You truly "light up my life."

Finally, thanks be to God, who has blessed me with the light of the gospel of grace. My faith and righteousness is built solely on Christ, the solid rock. To Him be all the glory. And may He be pleased to bring many into saving relationship with Himself through this book.

Contents

Where Do We Stand Today? 9

Part One: The Historical Heritage

1. The Holy Catholic Church 15
2. The Dark Ages? 25
3. The Great Evangelical Recovery 41
4. A Fallen Church? 55

Part Two: The Theological Issues

5. The Central Mystery of the Christian Faith? 73
6. Seven Sacraments? 90
7. Who Really Speaks for God? 103
8. Spiritual Life and Devotion 119
9. Death and the Life to Come 138

Part Three: The Challenge Today

10. The Present Hour 153
11. Is Evangelical Really Enough? 168
12. Recovering Biblical Christianity 184

A Personal Invitation 201
Notes 205
For Further Reading 211
Answers to Quiz 214

Where Do We Stand Today?

This book was originally birthed in response to a perceived need in the present church scene. In 1993 I was asked to edit a volume of academic essays written by several evangelical scholars and intended for serious study by those who wanted to better understand modern Catholicism. This previous book, titled *Roman Catholicism: Evangelical Protestants Analyze What Divides and Unites Us* (Moody Press, 1994), became a survey of modern Catholic faith and practice, written from an evangelical perspective. In preparing this academic book I wanted to enter into dialogue with Catholic thought without the acrimonious tone of past Catholic/Protestant debate. I realized then, and realize even more so now, that many, on both sides, do not like my approach. All of us find it difficult to honestly discuss our differences without becoming defensive and hostile. Sadly, Christians often get along better with those who profess no faith in Christ at all than with those who profess faith differently. On both sides there are many who will think my approach will surely result in compromise by the very definition of things.

It will become readily apparent that I do not think compromise is a real option. There are many vital truths that Catholics and evangelicals share in common. More and more we are discovering how vital these important beliefs we share in common really are. This is a world increasingly turned against historic and confessional Christianity. The "fresh winds" of ecumenism have produced a new openness among believers from nearly every quarter of the world. All of this is good. We all must long for better days of true good will, especially among those who claim to follow the Prince of Peace.

At the same time I believe we need to honestly reconsider the vital differences that remain between evangelicals and Roman Catholics. All of the good intentions of present efforts for unity will not make our important differences vanish. We all have much to learn in humbly following Christ in the spirit of His gospel. I have been a follower of Jesus Christ for well over 40 years and sometimes I still feel as if I have only just begun. My library is well stocked with books by both Roman Catholics and evangelicals. I have benefited much by reading theology from both sides. There is still much to be understood.

I believe evangelicals need to appreciate more seriously the great traditions of historic Christianity. There is something very important that *serious* Catholics and *serious* evangelicals hold in common—historic orthodoxy. One of the great weaknesses of modern evangelicalism is that it has progressively cut itself off from the historical confessions and practices of the church down through the centuries.

At the same time a great weakness in Catholicism has been its failure to study seriously and wrestle carefully with the teachings of the Bible itself. (Thankfully a new generation of Catholic scholarship has begun to produce some very impressive biblical thought.) No matter how lovely the liturgical elements of Catholicism might be, in helping lift the human soul Godward in real reverence, these can never replace the need for Holy Scripture.

Because of the more academic nature of my earlier book, and because of the tone and daunting size of several dozen more popular books, this book has been published. It is written with the hope that it will invite the average person into the discussion of the Catholic mystery as understood by an evangelical writer who truly loves and respects Catholics. Throughout this book I try to speak to Catholics as a friend would speak to a friend. I have no animosity in how I approach my subject. Personally, I have discovered prejudice on both sides of the evangelical/Catholic divide. What I desire is *serious dialogue* with modern Catholic belief and practice. I want to understand the mystery that is Roman Catholicism and I want to test that mystery at all points by the Scriptures.

I also want to help evangelical readers better understand what is happening within modern Catholicism and demonstrate why certain biblical and evangelical beliefs are still extremely important. If I understand the present moment in history, these are extremely important times. While Western culture fails morally and politically, the church stands as perhaps the only citadel of righteousness in nations once deeply influenced by Catholic and Protestant faith. The call for us to share together in opposition to morally destructive positions, such as abortion on demand and infidelity, is right and good. But such a call, to what has been rightly termed "mere Christianity," must never blur the essential truth of the gospel itself. There are some very important beliefs and practices where Catholics and evangelicals still differ. It is time we discussed these without rancor.

Perhaps modern times will yield a new form of agreement not seen in the past. I pray that this might be the case. But I pray even more that the gospel of God's grace will again be central to a revitalized church in the new millennium. Though this book will primarily focus the reader's attention on those beliefs and practices that still genuinely divide Catholics and evangelicals, my greater concern is that members of every church will come to trust in Jesus Christ alone. Only here is true assurance and peace with God.

Our greatest common concern has to be the presence of relativism in all our ranks—the idea that truth changes from one person to the next. This soul-destroying philosophy has eaten like a canker into all modern expressions of Christian faith, Catholic and evangelical alike.

John Wesley, an ardent evangelist and Christian writer, published a letter to a Roman Catholic (in Dublin in 1749) in which he states the spirit with which I write:

> I do not suppose all the bitterness is on your side. I know there is too much on our side also. So much I fear that many Protestants (so-called) will be angry at me, too, for writing to you in this manner, and will say, "'Tis showing you too much favour; you deserve no such treatment at our hands." . . . I shall therefore endeavour, as mildly and inoffensively as I can, to remove in some measure the ground of your unkindness by plainly declaring what our belief and what our practice is.

In the spirit of the famous John Wesley I propose to enter into an irenic search for understanding *The Catholic Mystery*. I invite you to prayerfully join me.

PART 1

The Historical Heritage

The Christian church was not always divided by many of the barriers and disagreements that now exist. Though persecutions threatened to destroy the young church, she grew stronger with every wave of attack. Heresies and schisms threatened her almost from the beginning, but the visible church remained virtually one until a great division between East and West in the eleventh century.

In the sixteenth century another great division came to the Western church when Rome, then the political and religious center of the magisterial church, excommunicated an Augustinian monk named Martin Luther and set off the Protestant Reformation. Finally, at the Council of Trent (1545–1563), Rome closed the door to the theological contributions of the Reformers, who sought to correct serious errors that had evolved over the previous two centuries.

What brought about this great divide, and why is it that most evangelicals today will not simply "go home to Rome" now that Vatican II has offered an olive branch by naming Protestants "separated brethren"?

CHAPTER ONE

The Holy Catholic Church

I believe in God the Father Almighty, Maker of heaven and earth; and in Jesus Christ His only Son, our Lord, who was conceived by the Holy Spirit, born of the virgin Mary, suffered under Pontius Pilate, was crucified, dead, and buried; He descended into hell; the third day He rose from the dead; He ascended into heaven, and sitteth on the right hand of God the Father Almighty; from thence He shall come to judge the living and the dead.

I believe in the Holy Spirit; the holy catholic church, the communion of saints; the forgiveness of sins; the resurrection of the body; and the life everlasting. Amen.

These are the familiar words of the Apostles' Creed, a historic and simple summary of the most basic truths confessed by early Christians. Though this confession is most certainly not the direct product of the 12 apostles of Christ, it is commonly agreed that this short creed is a summary statement of the apostles' teaching. It is plainly in harmony with the spirit of the New Testament.

Most Catholics know this creed well. They are often surprised to hear Protestants quote it. Likewise, some evangelicals are equally surprised when they hear fellow evangelicals recite it. Often evangelicals are even more surprised to discover that here is an ancient creed that is not so much an abstract and mysterious document as a living, vibrant, profession of essential truths believed by all Christians across the centuries.

Here we have a universal starting point for Christian affirmation—a creed which expresses vital, foundational Christian truths confessed by believers long before the rupture of the visible church in the eleventh and sixteenth centuries. But all that needs to be confessed by modern Christians is not in this creed. Nothing, for example, regarding the grace of God in salvation is found in this creed. And nothing touching upon the authority of Scripture is found here either. Nevertheless, this is a good beginning—a starting point for all historic Christian confession. Here we have an illustration of what C. S. Lewis, the famous Oxford writer, meant by "mere Christianity."

Living trust in Christ requires that Christian faith be rooted in history as well as in present experience. True confession cannot exist without the New Testament itself, and the New Testament requires that we confess allegiance to Christ, both to His person and His work. All who profess love for Christ need to understand this. "But wait a minute," you say. "I am an evangelical Christian. I cannot confess that I believe in the 'holy catholic church.' That language is not acceptable to me. I believe in a biblical New Testament church, but not a 'holy catholic church.'"

Through the centuries believers have always confessed their faith by asserting belief in the holy catholic church. This is not anti-evangelical language. It was our Lord who constituted His church as a holy catholic church when He said, "I will build My church, and the gates of Hades will not overcome it" (Matthew 16:18). This often disputed text asserts that Jesus is committed to His church. Because the church is

His, it is holy, or "set apart" from ordinary purposes. Because it is a church spread over the whole earth, encompassing peoples of every background, both ethnically and socially (see Revelation 5:9), it is a catholic (meaning "universal") church.

When we use the words *Roman Catholic*, however, we are talking about something else; namely, a communion linked to the historic authority and practice of Rome. That is why the abbreviated name *Catholic* is properly capitalized when it is used in this book with reference to the Roman Catholic Church. In this case *Catholic* is being used of a particular communion of people, not as a reference to all Christians who make up the universal, or catholic, church of Christ.

One Faith . . . One Lord . . . One Church?

The apostle Paul confessed the affirmation "one body [church] and one Spirit . . . one Lord, one faith" (Ephesians 4:4-5). Though Christians clearly have differing beliefs of what the visible church should look like, they all agree there is a universal church in the world. (This simple observation is not meant to gloss over some very significant differences between differing views regarding the *essence* of the church.)

The word *Catholic* (when referring to Roman Catholicism) is a relatively recent term. Until the sixteenth century it was simply "the church." Sometimes it would be "the church catholic." Not until some years after the Protestant Reformation did the church, historically based in Rome, begin to use the title *Catholic* to distinguish itself from the Protestant movement. The church, headquartered in Vatican City, with its argument for succession of apostles back to Peter, came to be called the Roman Catholic Church. This name distinguished it not only from European Protestantism but from another historical branch of Christendom—the Eastern Orthodox Church, with its many similarities to the Roman Catholic

Church, excepting particularly its loyalty to the papacy and the requirement of celibacy for its priests.

> Resolved, that in the same spirit we propose no new creed, but taking broad, historical, and Evangelical catholic ground, we solemnly reaffirm and profess our faith in all the doctrines of the inspired word of God, and in the consensus of doctrines as held by all true Christians from the beginning. And we do more especially affirm our belief in the divine-human person and atoning work of our Lord and Savior Jesus Christ as the only and sufficient source of salvation, as the heart and soul of Christianity and as the center of all true Christian union and fellowship.[1]

The World Evangelical Fellowship, formed in our present century, represents various associations of regional and national fellowships of evangelical churches. It stands in the same tradition of thought by confessing, in part, the following: "We believe in . . . the unity of the Spirit of all true believers, the church, the body of Christ."

What is meant by these evangelical Christian affirmations when they speak of the church as *catholic*? And what is meant by the modifiers "broad, historical, and Evangelical catholic ground" used in the above statement? To answer that question we need to consider the doctrinal unity that developed in the historic church during the first five centuries following the death of Christ and the apostles.

The Historic Consensus: Its Importance

The visible church of Jesus Christ sought from its very beginning to maintain its essential oneness in teaching and life. In the midst of a hostile and anti-Christian culture, this was vital to its strength. Opposition from outside the church threatened it with intense periods of persecution as various Roman emperors came and went over the centuries. Ten bloody seasons of persecution resulted.

The overall effect of these attempts to stop the growth of the church was a continual purifying of the church from nominal professions of faith. This ultimately brought deep and lasting growth in both power and influence. As the old saying goes, "The blood of the martyrs was the seed of the church!"

What threatened the church even more in those early centuries was error from within. The infant movement was threatened with compromise and heresy. The visible body of Christ on earth was distressed repeatedly by serious heresies. What did the leadership of the young church do to counteract these insidious viruses within her?

Over the first four centuries a number of councils were convened to address these doctrinal errors. Bishops (presbyters, or leaders of churches and groups of churches) met at important cities for months at a time to consider important doctrinal and moral issues facing the church. Some of these councils were called for political reasons. Others became, quite honestly, platforms for leaders whose motives were not always noble. Yet through it all, God's providence overruled. God the Holy Spirit was at work guiding the church into a fuller and deeper understanding of the essential truths that would protect the message of Christ and His apostles from errors that would destroy it.

It is not surprising that in the early centuries the church addressed these kinds of problems so directly. Had not the apostle Paul written, "By the grace God has given me, I laid a foundation as an expert builder, and someone else is building on it. But each one should be careful how he builds. For no one can lay any foundation other than the one already laid, which is Jesus Christ" (1 Corinthians 3:10-11)? The foundation of the church was Christ. About this there must be no lingering doubt. What made Christianity a vital religion in the ancient Roman culture was the uniqueness of its founder—both His unique person and His unique work. To build on any foundation other than Christ Jesus was, simply put, to invite disaster. It was to build with wood, hay, and straw rather than gold, silver, and costly stones (see verse 12).

The early history of the church followed Paul's pattern. It built a solid confessional foundation. This foundation was laid by these early councils and creeds. Affirmation followed affirmation, and denial followed denial. These all were necessary if the church was to be faithful to the work of the apostles—namely, the New Testament Scriptures themselves.

Perhaps the greatest example of what I have in mind can be observed in the work of the church council that met at Chalcedon in late 451. After 15 difficult sessions the 520 bishops succeeded in drafting a creed that answered the important theological questions of that day—such as the relationship of divinity and humanity in the person of Jesus. The church had previously affirmed (in 325 and 381) that Jesus was "God of very God" and "of the same substance" as the Father. But by the late fifth century new questions had arisen. If Jesus was fully divine, how could He still be human? And if He was both human and divine, how did the humanity and divinity exist in one and the same person?

Historian Mark Noll has noted something of the significance of these events:

> As it had at the Council of Nicaea and Constantinople, so at Chalcedon the church took up questions of ultimate importance concerning the person and work of Christ. In the broader sweep of church history, Chalcedon showed that it was possible, through judicious use of one era's dominant forms of thought, to define critical aspects of Christianity as handed down in the Scriptures. Moreover, Chalcedon showed that such necessary theological work can succeed despite an environment of brutal ecclesiastical strife and despite the reality of cultural division within the church itself. In these terms Chalcedon was a threefold triumph of Christian catholicity over cultural fragmentation, and a triumph of discriminating theological reasoning over the anti-intellectual dismissal of philosophy, on the one

hand, and over a theological capitulation to philosophy, on the other.[2]

Similar historic councils during the first seven centuries addressed matters such as the discipline of ministers, schism, and doctrinal heresies, but the principal heresies addressed in those early centuries were those that dealt with the person of Jesus Christ. Was He really God? Was He truly man? How are we to understand the triune nature of the Godhead in light of Christ being eternal God, yet distinct from the Father, who is also eternal God? And what is the relationship of the Holy Spirit to the Father and the Son? The answers the church formed are the doctrinal material of historic orthodoxy, both Catholic and evangelical.

Roman Catholics and Evangelicals

Catholics and evangelicals share a consistent loyalty to the creeds of the early orthodox fathers and theologians. When the Protestant Reformation took place in the sixteenth century, there was never a serious battle over any of the great truths that had united the church for centuries. And there is still much that we share together in these bedrock foundational beliefs, especially in an age that has launched an attack upon all truth claims.

Since the turn of the twentieth century, however, large segments of Protestantism have turned away from these historic Christian statements of faith. In more recent years this same liberal virus has infected Catholic theologians and, with them, many parish priests as well. We live in an era quite different from the way things used to be. In the past we could have assumed that all Catholics and Protestants agreed on the orthodox creedal statements of the first five or six centuries. But that has changed. Modernist ministers and priests have jettisoned truths once held by all who named Christ in our respective traditions. And this development has confused many church members.

Our young people often go away to Catholic and Protestant schools only to have essential Christian truths undermined by professors who are financially supported by the families and churches of these children. What is happening? A twentieth-century error has influenced both Catholics and evangelicals. It attacks almost everything previously assumed as part and parcel of the historic Christian faith. This error has caused many Catholics and evangelicals to realize that we have a new common enemy. Both secularism and materialism threaten to bring down Western culture. Moral chaos abounds, both in personal lives and in society at large. And the pluralistic dimensions of a more liberal ecumenism threaten all our respective Christian distinctives.

Evangelical historian Mark Noll, in showing how our histories in this century have brought us closer to one another, cites the *diversity* that exists in our respective communities as the actual basis for an increasingly significant ground for common concern. He notes that British historian David Bebbington has cited four marks of modern evangelicalism that have the tendency to unite those who properly fit this category of Christian expression—conversionism, activism, biblicism, and crucicentrism. Concludes Noll, "From the Protestant side . . . it is necessary to use extreme care in speaking about the often diverse elements that fit under the category 'evangelical.'"[3] Noll correctly observes that this existence of diverse elements

> . . . is almost equally true from the other side as well. Despite persisting tendencies to speak of a unified Catholic movement, such efforts are now nearly as indefensible as similar generalities applied to Protestants. Catholics do retain a structural unity symbolized by the pope and the Church's hierarchy, but it would be wise for Protestants to let Catholics say what that structure means. Speaking as a

> Catholic theologian, Richard McBrien can say of the current scene, "There are sometimes sharper divisions within the Roman Catholic Church than there are between certain Catholics and certain Protestants." . . . Given the situation of religious pluralism within the Christian families, there is much more opportunity than even fifty years ago to find meaningful fellowship across, as well as significant strife within, traditional evangelical and Catholic communities.[4]

In the face of a contemporary pluralistic challenge, especially in Europe and the United States, Catholics and evangelicals are increasingly talking about the common enemies of their faith. We are finding out that we agree on most of the writings of the early church fathers and the councils and creeds of Christendom. This generally comes as a surprise to lay people on both sides of the Reformation. The result has been a growing awareness of our need to work together in areas where we are being attacked by forces that are distinctly related to modern and postmodern life.

Summing Up

Evangelicals need to better understand that we confess a continuity of truth through the ages and that these early church creeds are gifts to us. Certainly we should subject them to the authority of Scripture, as we will see in chapter 5, but we believe that much of what Scripture teaches, especially regarding the nature of God and Christ, *is plainly defended and set forth* by these ancient creeds.

Evangelicals share more than a few vital biblical truths with Catholics. We seek to cultivate a *distinctly* Christian worldview. We both believe—if we reject the modernist criticism now present in our respective traditions—that the Bible is the infallible Word of God. We are consistent supernaturalists who believe in the doctrines of the Trinity, the deity and humanity of Christ, and the bodily resurrection of Christ. We confess faith in His ascension into heaven and in His future bodily return. We believe in life after the grave and in the judgment that follows. We even sing some of the same songs, use the same biblical texts in our public worship, practice intercessory prayer, and develop a spiritual life grounded on faith in Christ.

Catholics need to better understand that evangelicals are not radicals who broke away from the ancient faith of the church. Luther, Calvin, and the early Protestant Reformers strongly affirmed their loyalty to the creeds and went far to demonstrate that they were true heirs of the early church. This is precisely why we still have so much in common. Evangelical faith is not novel. It is not anti-catholic, given how the historic church has understood catholicism. The Reformers never dreamed of "throwing out" historic affirmations in whole or in part.

What the early Protestant Reformers did do was to challenge a church authority they believed contradicted itself. There is a world of difference in both spirit and practice between reactionaries and reformers. They believed, quite simply, that the visible church had gone beyond the authority of Scripture. They further asserted that the gospel had been lost through the evolution of medieval doctrine. This evolution so corrupted the visible church, according to the Reformers, that *complete reformation* in vital areas of faith and practice was the only solution.

In this book we will consider what caused this Reformation and what doctrinal areas were at the heart of the divide. We will then ask, "Does it still matter?" and, further, "How should evangelicals and Catholics address these differences in a new atmosphere that invites better understanding and greater tolerance?"

CHAPTER TWO

The Dark Ages?

As the church moved beyond the early centuries into the era of the medieval world, several things began to change, both in the world and in the church. In this chapter we will consider these shifts and how they prepared the way for a great divide that would come in the sixteenth century.

Evangelicals often think of the medieval era as a time of total spiritual darkness across much of Europe. It is thought that the church was cold, lifeless, and dead. That the true story is quite different surprises many evangelicals.

It must be understood that the Christianity of the Middle Ages, at least in Europe, developed into what has been called Christendom. Christendom was a result of what has been called "the medieval synthesis." This "synthesis" harmonized, in theory, the sacred and secular aspects of everyday life. The Christian faith profoundly influenced politics, social order, and economics, as well as religious devotion. This influence was primarily grounded in the faith as taught by the bishop in Rome.

Though the light of true faith flickered dimly at times, it never died. John Scotus Erigena, described by many as the one true original thinker of the Dark Ages, was also a great philosopher-theologian. Though theology became generally confined to the monasteries during this long period, the goal was *not* knowledge for its own sake, but knowledge that resulted in devotion and worship. Theology in this era, an era so unlike our postmodern age, was not done by *detached* thinkers but by *committed* followers.

The central conviction of the theology of this time period may surprise some evangelicals. Human beings, the church confessed consistently, were totally corrupted by sin, needed a real salvation, and this salvation could come only through the meritorious accomplishments of Christ. And this work of Christ came to the sinner on the basis of God's grace alone. Historian Mark Noll notes, cryptically, that "the distinctive medieval shape of these convictions was the belief that saving grace comes to people through the sacraments in a social setting defined by the cooperation of church and state."[1]

At this point many evangelicals react without an understanding of either the what or the why of these developments. Let me develop this thought a bit further.

Sacramental theology clearly evolved during the centuries of the Middle Ages. This evolution came to full flower in the theological contributions of the great theologian Thomas Aquinas, who said a sacrament was "the sign of a holy thing insofar as it makes men holy."[2] This meant, simply, the sacraments stood for *spiritual realities* and they *contributed* to the salvation of those who received them in faith through vital relationship to Christ through His church.

A widely respected church historian concludes:

> The theological rationale for a comprehensive sacramental system involved some elements shared by all times and places in Christian history and some that were distinct to Christendom in the Middle Ages. In the first place, the sacraments were thought to exhibit the principles of the incarnation, whereby the most important spiritual realities were embodied in a material form. Next, sacraments were thought to

> express the objective character of God's action on behalf of humanity. Receiving God's grace depended upon actually receiving the vehicle of that grace, and not so much on how one felt about the transaction. Finally, the sacraments were held to reinforce the essentially social structure of grace, the fact that Christ worked for his people together. This belief especially heightened the significance of the institutional church, through which the sacraments were given.[3]

By the eleventh century, with the emergence of reason as a method to be utilized in theology, the church entered into a whole new writing phase. The results of this were initially quite positive. Men such as Anselm, Abelard, and Bernard of Clairvaux (the last great representative of the monastic era) produced a considerable corpus of material that brought further light upon and deeper consideration to several great theological truths. But by the thirteenth century, theology, and the church with it, embarked upon a new and more dangerous phase. Philosophy, which had entered into the theological process as a servant tool, now developed into several new rival systems of thought. Dangers were on the horizon.

Through all this we must remember that in the early centuries the church was a persecuted minority. By the time it entered the medieval world it had evolved into either an aggressive proponent of the establishment or, at the very least, a major player in the political and social systems of the time. This shift had begun with the conversion of Emperor Constantine in the early fourth century. By the eighth and ninth centuries, the church had won its battle with pagan culture and its thought and life became associated with the cause of victory. The persecuted little flock was now a victorious army, trampling down pagan ideas that lay before it. *Christus Victor* became more than a theological truth; it was a summary of the church's actual status in the world. This victory clearly brought with it a distinct theological emphasis—the language of victory over the devil, sin, and death. It also brought with it related problems of ecclesiastical triumphalism, a kind of celebrative spirit connected with victory over others.

Regarding these developments, church historian D. Clair Davis concludes, "Though conditioned by the church's history, this theology of the early church faithfully reflected an important aspect of the biblical teaching of salvation. It stressed redemption—how God delivers His people from their bondage into the freedom of life with Him."[4]

As the old Roman Empire broke up and more familial ways of thinking and living developed in Europe, people became concerned about right thinking regarding their personal relationship to God and to the church. As surely as the doctrines of God, Christ, man, and sin had occupied the attention of the early centuries, so now the church would address, in a more focused way, the doctrine of salvation. How was the great disruption between man and God to be resolved? How did man enter into fellowship with an offended, holy God?

All this led to considerable discussion of the doctrine of the atonement—the nature and design of Christ's death and how God redeems lost human beings—by the church's best theologians. The development of the church's thinking followed a discernible path—from God and Christ, to humanity and sin, and finally to grace and salvation.

Humanity's fall, and the depraved nature that resulted from it, as well as the need for divine grace, had all been debated at length in Augustine's response to Pelagius. Augustine, a bishop in North Africa, was an important theologian. Pelagius, also a significant figure in this era, was a fifth-century heretic who denied the necessity of sovereign grace in salvation because he failed to properly understand the biblical teaching of the bondage of the human will to sin. In the end, Pelagius, like some in our time, reasoned that "if it's going to be it's up to me." He held the widely popular notion that in the matter of salvation "God helps those who help themselves." The reason St. Augustine became the champion of reigning grace was that he so clearly understood the nature of sin and its effects upon human beings. And the church followed Augustine's doctrine for centuries to come.

Two Theologians of Importance

Anselm, the Archbishop of Canterbury (ca. 1033–1109), is perhaps best known for his insistence that Christian reason must trace its journey back to faith in Christ in order to determine what it knows and understands. Philosophic speculation could not help the church unless it was submitted properly to faith. By this he meant, simply, "I do not seek to understand that I may believe, but I believe that I may understand: for this I also believe, that unless I believe I will not understand." Anselm contributed significantly to the historically developing doctrine of the atonement. He argued in his classic book *Cur Deus Homo* (*Why the God-Man*?) from the facts of the incarnation and the cross back to God's purpose in sending Christ and the reason for His death. The uniqueness of the person who died at Calvary requires that the event—that is, His sacrificial death—be unique as well. Only Christ as the God-man could bear the wrath of God and pay the full penalty of sin. Because God is holy, sin violates His honor. Because His honor is violated, His wrath is consistently just and totally perfect. Because of His wrath, sinners must have a perfect atonement made for them.

As in many theological conflicts through the ages, orthodox views often engender rival views. In the case of Anselm, his chief antagonist was Peter Abelard (1079–1142). Abelard was a scholastic philosopher and theologian who sought to reconcile faith and reason. For Abelard "the value of the atonement was in the individual's personal response to what Christ had done for him. As he came to appreciate and bow in gratitude at the extent of God's love for him, he would respond in turn with his own love to the God who had loved him so much."[5]

Does God require satisfaction, or payment, in order for sin to be atoned for? Or is the cross merely a display of God's love, a point of persuasive appeal for people to trust Christ? Put another way, is the cross a place where God *actually* redeems lost men and women by atoning for their sin?

Evangelical Christians have always insisted that the love of God is demonstrated by the cross. Many of our hymns reveal this truth (for example, "There Is a Green Hill Far Away," "Rock of Ages," "Alas! And Did My Savior Bleed," "He Was Wounded for Our Transgressions"). But we also insist, with Anselm and his theological tradition, that the love of Calvary is not simply a generic display of deep affection for humanity. It is a specific and particular action taken by God to actually remove His holy wrath from those He saves through the death of His Son. This is done by the Father, mysteriously, when He pours out all His wrath upon His own unique Son. In 1875 hymn writer Philip P. Bliss captured this undestanding well when he wrote these words:

"Man of Sorrows!" what a name
For the Son of God who came
Ruined sinners to reclaim!
Hallelujah! what a Savior!

Bearing shame and scoffing rude,
In my place condemned He stood;
Sealed my pardon with His blood;
Hallelujah! what a Savior!

Guilty, vile, and helpless we;
Spotless Lamb of God was He;
"Full atonement!" can it be?
Hallelujah! what a Savior!

Lifted up was He to die,
"It is finished," was His cry;
Now in heav'n exalted high;
Hallelujah! what a Savior!

"What Must I Do to Be Saved?"

People must be brought face to face with God's wrath and their own sin. When, by the Spirit, this happens, they cry in deep anguish, "What must I do to be saved?" (see Acts 16:30). Salvation, biblically understood, is rescue and deliverance. But what exactly must we be saved from?

A simple answer is at hand—we must be saved from sin. But what is sin? Sin is a violation of the moral law of God (1 John 3:4, "sin is lawlessness"). The law is revealed to us through Holy Scripture and human conscience. All of us fail to conform to the law of God (see Romans 3:23). This failure is attended by the gravest of penalties (Ezekiel 18:4,20, "The soul who sins is the one who will die"). But sin is more than action alone. It even extends to motives. God can, and does, judge the heart (Hebrews 4:13, "Nothing in all creation is hidden from God's sight. Everything is uncovered and laid bare before the eyes of him to whom we must give account"). And further we read, "There is no one righteous, not even one; there is no one who understands, no one who seeks God. All have turned away, they have together become worthless, there is no one who does good, not even one" (Romans 3:10-12).

The Bible makes it plain (see 1 John 1:8) that no one, not even the most deliberately dedicated Christian, can ever live, at least this side of the kingdom to come, without the problem of sin. So what is the solution? The apostle John said we must have our sins "forgiven." We must be "cleansed from all unrighteousness." Scripture indicates that there are three things necessary for solving this sin problem: 1) There must be a *means* for cleansing us from all sin—the blood of Christ (1 John 1:7); 2) there must be a *method* for cleansing us from all sin—personal confession (1 John 1:9); and 3) there must be a definite *measure* of forgiveness and cleansing (as noted)—we are cleansed of *all* unrighteousness when we trust the One who intercedes for us and is our advocate (see 1 John 2:1-2).

During the Middle Ages the church developed a particular way of understanding and practicing the truth of Scripture regarding forgiveness. It sought to apply an objective theology of the atonement to the subjective question, "How can I lay hold of what Christ has done in His death? How can I make this event my own?"

As we noted earlier, over the preceding centuries the church had answered this question by increasingly encouraging penitent believers to look to the mystery of the sacraments. The sacraments were objective. They pointed outside the penitent to God's grace, so they were believed. The reasoning process eventually looked something like this: Christ had died. He had given all authority to the bishops of the church, especially to the bishop of Rome, who some argued was Peter's successor. (This was not universally believed at first.) Here, in Peter's place, was the power to bind and loose people from their sins. This power was then conferred upon the bishops, who in turn gave it to the priests who ultimately presided over the sacraments in the life of the church.

The sacrament of baptism, where grace was first received, was the critical mystery. It brought one into a saving relationship with Christ and His church. The Supper (or Mass, as it was eventually called) was the central channel of continuing salvation for all baptized believers who wished to receive grace and remain savingly united with Christ. But receiving the Mass would not, in itself, save a person. There must be true faith and repentance in the heart. Grace must be received in a proper (worthy) manner. But all of this implies that salvation comes by human effort, in some manner, not by grace. As a result of this type of thought, medieval theologians developed what was conceived of as an indispensable sacrament for coming properly to the Mass—penance.

In penance the faithful had their repentance made whole and complete. Inadequate repentance was changed—through penance it became heartfelt, real, complete. The same was true for faith. Small or weak faith—we might even say superficial faith—became genuine faith *through* penance. This transformation might not even be perceptible, but it was, nonetheless, real. And it was to play a vital role in the developing mystery called Christianity.

This whole concept, which had developed in the Monastic movement, wherein men consecrated themselves to a life of sacrifice and suffering, was intended to help people fulfill Paul's injunction to "put off" the old life and "put on" the new life (see Colossians 3:8-17). The concern was to make sure that the recipients of grace would truly follow on in obedience once they began their Christian journey.

Penance was intended to change behavior, but in time it became identified with punishment for what the confessing person had already done. In many ways it became a virtual synonym for repentance, but with a much more legalistic bent. People began to travel to holy sites to observe ancient relics and in general to strive for greater holiness in order to receive grace. Eventually substitute penances were devised that relied on a monetary payment to the church. These were called indulgences. (We will see the importance of this development a bit later.) Such indulgences were often used for the removal of future sins.

In the twelfth, thirteenth, and fourteenth centuries, just prior to the rise of the Protestant Reformation, two contrasting emphases arose in the church: mysticism and sacramentalism. Mysticism flourished particularly in Germany. The herald of this movement was Meister Eckhart, who died in 1327. Eckhart taught that external moral acts will *not* sanctify us and cannot, therefore, contribute to our salvation. His ideas were developed by churchmen such as John Ruysbroeck (1293–1381), John Tauler (d. 1361), and Henry Suso

(1295–1366). Ruysbroeck, as an example, described true religion as man's hunt, with the Holy Ghost as the hound, for the divine. Tauler insisted that man must surrender the transitory, destroy his self-will, and surrender himself completely to the Holy Spirit. The pattern of these mystics is one followed through many centuries: 1) purification, 2) illumination, and 3) unification. This emphasis produced one of the great little classics of Christian literature, *The Imitation of Christ*, by Thomas à Kempis.

In contrast to this mystical strand stressing direct personal experience with God and grace there was an externalizing emphasis that took shape through sacramentalism. In time most of the clergy would follow this path. After all, saying an Ave Maria over and over was a much easier substitute for keeping the law of God. As a result the sacrament of penance, described earlier, took on inordinate importance. The constant duty of the sinner was to confess his sins to the parish priest and then do necessary works of satisfaction. Fear of punishment (attrition) was enough to satisfy the church, according to many. All of this tended to displace genuine penitence (contrition) and heartfelt sorrow for sin. The works of satisfaction that were intended to follow confession and absolution were, ultimately, too much for most people to bear. The church, by the fourteenth and fifteenth centuries, began to provide easier substitutes for the masses of people.

D. Clair Davis is helpful once again. He summarizes the problem well:

> Technically, only the temporal penalty for sin was being dealt with (the punishment due sin this side of eternity, including that endured in purgatory), but for practical purposes that was all that anyone knew about anyway. Knowledge that one's eternal punishment had been dealt with (the assurance of salvation) was available in any case only to those few—the saints to whom it had been revealed by extraordinary revelation. The gap that penance was de-

vised to bridge was, in the end, still a great chasm: How can a weak sinner come to a holy Christ?[6]

First, the medieval church said a person was saved by receiving grace in the Mass *if* the person had sincere faith and repentance. But when the penitent asked the question, "Is my faith and repentance sincere?" he could not know for sure. To solve this problem, he added penance. But what if his penance was incomplete, his faith not genuinely holy? The answer was this: If his or her faith was at least sincere, he would be granted what was called "congruous grace"—the grace God gives to those who are sincerely trying to please Him. "But how can I know that I am sincere?" is the next question that arises. With this approach, there can be no real assurance of salvation. The great theologian Augustine had written of election and predestination, of an invisible church made up of those who truly know the grace of God. "But how can I know that I am truly a part of the body of Christ?"

What resulted from all this was the desire to do one's best with the most sincere effort possible. Unintentionally, salvation became the joining of grace *and* human effort. And theology, the study of God and His revelation, appeared as "unknowable . . . an irrelevant puzzle."[7]

The Problem of Indulgences

All this led to the spark that finally lit the fire of the Reformation—the sale and commercialization of indulgences. The story goes like this: An itinerant preacher, John Tetzel, came to Germany (1517) offering indulgences to the zealous crowds with great flair. Luther had seen enough. He later noted that Tetzel preached crass ideas such as:

- If St. Peter were present, he would have no greater grace and authority than he (i.e., Tetzel) had.

- Tetzel insisted that he had no desire to exchange places with St. Peter, for he had saved more souls with indulgences than Peter had with preaching.
- When a man deposited money in Tetzel's coffers, a soul left purgatory for heaven as soon as the coin touched the bottom of the chest.
- And, remorse and sorrow were not necessary for repentance from sin if a man bought an indulgence.

Historians, both Catholic and Protestant, agree that when Luther first raised doubts regarding these indulgences he had no intention of leaving the church. He regarded this matter as symptomatic of general sickness within the church of his time. His *Ninety-five Theses* of October 1517, written in Latin for the purpose of discussion by scholars, circulated widely within two weeks. As early as 1518, when Luther was interrogated by Cardinal Cajetan at Augsburg, it was made very clear that he was alienating himself from the Roman church. What is even more interesting is that as we look back over this story, we can't help but notice that Luther's statements were not new at all. At various times during the previous two centuries scholastic theologians had raised virtually the same questions Luther was asking.

So what was the real problem? For sure Luther objected to the avarice and fund raising associated with the sale of indulgences. In time, even Catholic reformers would admit to these errors. Luther also protested the notion that buying an indulgence could contribute anything to one's salvation, or that of a loved one. His chief objection, however, was to the principle of indulgences themselves, *not* simply to the abuse. As has been accurately noted: "The crux of the *Ninety-five Theses* was the premise that the church can remit only penances imposed by itself, and that this jurisdiction does not extend to the dead (theses 5, 8, 10-11, 13, 20-22, 34)."[8] This meant, in reality, that even the pope had no authority over souls in the next world, other than that of intercession. This line of argumentation had devastating implications for both the doctrine of purgatory and the papacy.

To understand this further we need, once again, a better comprehension of the medieval mindset behind it. If nothing else, the church was consistent with medieval theology in its development of the doctrine and practice of indulgences.

What, exactly, was behind the sale of indulgences to ordinary Catholics? The medieval church's definition of sin helps to answer this question. If a person died with mortal sin (murder, adultery, even missing Mass, and so on), he or she was on the road to perdition. Mortal sin kills the life of grace begun in baptism, though confession may bring back the life of grace. Unconfessed venial sins (lying, petty theft, unkind words, and so on) meant that the person would need to spend time in purgatory, a place for cleansing (purging) from remaining sin.

Since Vatican II many liberal Catholics have insisted that the use of indulgences was only a sixteenth-century practice. The truth of the matter seems contrary to this reforming wish. To a large extent indulgences still exist in many popular ways in today's Catholic Church (examples abound on the Catholic cable network, EWTN, and in 1985 the pope announced that indulgences could be received via television if the right conditions were met). A November 1998 *New York Times* religion report on "The Great Jubilee of the Year 2000" reveals that this practice is still very much a part of the Catholic mystery. The recent papal bull titled *Incarnationis Mysterium* (*The Mystery of the Incarnation*), formally issued on November 29, 1998, proclaims the year 2000 to be a Holy Year. This declaration actually serves as a practical guide to the mystery of salvation for faithful Catholics. The pope added that individual sinners (who met the proper conditions) would be granted "plenary indulgences," or a full pardon for sins, as opposed to a shortening of time spent in purgatory. The papacy listed, in its recent announcement, a wide variety of acts that can earn an indulgence. These range from a sacred pilgrimage to Rome, the Holy Land, or even to the cathedral or stipulated church in a given area. Acts of service to another, or even a day of abstaining from "unnecessary consumption" (including alcohol or tobacco), or donations to the poor, might also qualify.

Historically it was affirmed by the Catholic Church that all sins, even those confessed and absolved by the priest, incurred a debt of temporal punishment—that is, a finite amount of time to be spent in purgatory. It is here that indulgences came powerfully into the picture. Jesus Christ, the Blessed Mother, and the saints are all believed to have earned an abundance of merit through their holy lives. From this excess of stored merit believers might receive additional help. This help could be received through the mystery of Catholic faith and practice—for example, certain prayers, the veneration of relics, and the use of religious articles such as rosaries, crucifixes, and medals.

The indulgence, then, which included the operation and fulfillment of the sacramental act of penance, could be bought. The desire to escape punishment (which was very strong in those centuries), joined with the confession of sin to a priest and the purchase of an indulgence, all became the work of devoted followers of the church.

During the Middle Ages paying money to the church for indulgences not only brought divine help, but the money would assist the church in her mission work. It was the evolution of a particular doctrinal pattern, then, as well as the abuse of this practice, that led to the steps taken by Martin Luther—steps that precipitated the great divide in the Western church.

Perhaps the best way to understand Luther's true concern is to read the first two of his famous *Ninety-five Theses* just as he wrote them in late 1517:

1. When our Lord and Master Jesus Christ said, "Repent" [Matt. 4:17], he willed the entire life of believers to be one of repentance.

2. This word cannot be understood as referring to the sacrament of penance, that is, confession and satisfaction, as administered by the clergy.

Summing Up

The decline of medieval Christianity was very gradual. The more serious errors didn't arise until as late as the fourteenth and fifteenth centuries. Eventually the results of this descending darkness were serious. Even before Martin Luther in the early 1500s, Gregory of Rimini (a monk) and Thomas Bradwardine (the Archbishop of Canterbury) challenged the whole notion of *synthesis* in regard to salvation. What arose, because of these calls for reform, was a return by some theologians to Augustine's insistence upon the sovereignty of God's grace conquering people's sinful rebellion. These theologians reasoned that if a person relied upon sincere *cooperative* efforts with God and the church, then in the end it would not be grace that saved. Those who challenged popular thought viewed reliance upon various kinds of preparation for grace as forms of self-righteous human effort. God did not need help, even sincere human help, to save the sinner.

Out of this theological confusion, joined eventually with corrupt practices, the medieval church began to face serious abuses. So a providential historical context of criticism, which helped bring about the great change, was already in place when Luther began to speak out regarding the matter of indulgences.

Finally, Luther believed that there was one "only true indulgence" and that was the gospel of Jesus Christ itself. He came to this conclusion because of the plain meaning of Holy Scripture, which says, "Since we have now been justified by his blood, how much more shall we be saved from God's wrath through him!" (Romans 5:9). Modern evangelicals agree with this. Salvation is not found in indulgences, but through faith alone, in Christ alone, and without any human contribution whatsoever.

The changes that were needed in the sixteenth century eventually issued in a sad division. Catholics still think that this division was not necessary. Evangelicals, however, believe that the reforming of the historic Christian church led to this division because Catholicism refused to make necessary changes in both doctrine and practice.

CHAPTER THREE

The Great Evangelical Recovery

The sixteenth-century Reformation eventually became more than a movement for the purification of corrupt practices. It precipitated changes that forever altered the church. Some of the changes introduced were of immense importance. This is why it is much easier to discuss formal union between Roman Catholicism and Protestant church bodies in our own time than it is to actually make it happen in a confessional context. Several of the significant theological doctrines radically altered by the Protestant Reformation include:

- The Role of Scripture

The church, prior to the Reformation, had concluded that tradition, properly acknowledged by the church, was of equal authority with Scripture. The Reformers challenged this and affirmed that only 66 books made up the canon. In this decision they followed the recognized Hebrew canon of the Old Testament and rejected the Apocryphal books, which are still included in a Catholic version of Scripture. These Reformers did not deny the church's authority to teach God's Word nor did they reject tradition. What they insisted upon was that Holy Scripture alone was sufficient to function as the infallible rule (*regula fidei*) of faith for believers. This meant that *all* one must believe as a Christian is to be found in Scripture and that which is not found within Scripture, either directly or by clear inference, was nonbinding upon believing consciences. And with this they insisted that all tradition, even church tradition itself, must be subjected to the higher authority of the Bible.

■ The Doctrine of Man

Whereas Rome had taught, for several centuries, that sin corrupted mankind and predisposed all human persons to evil because of Adam, the Reformers stressed total or complete depravity, meaning that human nature was entirely affected by the fall. Further, the Reformers saw guilt as inherited from Adam. We sin because we *are* sinners. As a consequence all persons are in bondage to sin and their will is not able, in and of itself, to choose that which is good, including salvation.

■ The Doctrine of Salvation

Here is where the greatest changes of all came through the efforts of the Reformers. Rome had taught, through most of its major theologians in the previous three to five centuries, that prevenient grace, given at baptism, enabled a person to believe and cooperate with a free will. The Reformers insisted that even though common grace was given to all, only the elect were granted saving grace. In the Protestant view, good works were the result of grace, while in the Catholic view they were meritorious, contributing (by grace, it was argued) to salvation. For the Reformers, regeneration was the work of the Holy Spirit in calling the elect to faith, while Rome saw the grace of regeneration as infused by baptism.

Rome viewed the atonement of Christ's death as providing the merit of salvation, with its attendant blessings—while the blessings were passed on through the mystery of the sacraments. Protestant Reformers saw Christ's death as a substitutionary penal sacrifice. The most important of all differences was with regard to the doctrine of justification. Rome saw the forgiveness of sins as received at baptism and potentially lost through mortal sin. (It could be regained via penance!) The Reformers viewed justification as an objective, final, judicial act of God to rescue sinners *solely* on the basis of their trust, or faith, in the person and work of Christ.

■ The Doctrine of the Church

For many centuries it was argued that there was no salvation outside the visible church, which many concluded must be Rome. The Reformers, by contrast, made a distinction between the universal (invisible) church and the visible expression of the church, which could fall and needed continual correction by the Scriptures. Sacraments, for Rome, conveyed justifying and sanctifying grace *ex opere operato* (that is, by the operation it was done). Rome had seven such sacraments in its ecclesiastical order. Reformers, though they differed among themselves at some points, viewed the sacraments as only two in number and only as a means of grace when received by faith. Priests, for Rome, were actual mediators between God and man, while for the Reformers the doctrine of "the priesthood of all believers" was a theme of immense importance.

■ The Doctrine of the Future

As we noted in chapter 2, Luther's full-court press against indulgences caused him to undermine the doctrine of purgatory. Eventually he and the other Reformers rejected this idea altogether. Since they understood that true believers entered heaven upon death, and since they saw no clear text to be deduced in support of the doctrine of purgatory, they felt compelled to directly challenge this doctrinal belief.

Purgatory has always been a subject that stirs up intense feeling among those who accept or reject it. The idea is essentially this: most people, before they enter heaven, need to make some kind of atonement for temporal punishment that was not fully satisfactory while on earth. Even Catholic theologians have not agreed among themselves regarding some aspects of purgatory (for example, is the pain simply a loss of God and others, or does it involve actual physical torment as taught by the great theologian Aquinas?).

Historically, evangelicals have generally thought of the Protestant Reformation as a revival of historic Christianity. A serious doctrinal amnesia, however, has settled over many in our own day, with the result being a failure to appreciate this conclusion. Simply put—modern evangelicals are the heirs of this Reformation, but many have drifted quite far from its better contributions.

Roman Catholics, on the other hand, are inclined to think of the Reformation as a great disruption. They believe the Reformers, at best, *rejected* the church Christ established. Many believed, and some still believe, that this was actually a rejection of Christ Himself. "And over what?" Catholics ask. Practices that were later corrected by the Catholic Counter-Reformation itself, they reason. To devout Catholics, the Reformers' "rejection" seems to be a foolish choice.

I believe modern-day perceptions of the events of the sixteenth century are generally shallow and inadequate, both historically and theologically. Though the Reformation may have been ignited by Luther's challenges regarding indulgences, it very quickly became a sweeping challenge to the entire religious synthesis of the Middle Ages.

The Basis of the Challenge

The Reformers broke with Rome because they rejected the Christianity of the Middle Ages—a synthetic faith that failed to bring peace to their souls and the assurance of God's grace as the sole ground of their salvation. As they studied the text of the Greek New Testament, thanks to the scholarly work of Desiderius Erasmus, a Roman Catholic Renaissance humanist, they increasingly found Rome's message of salvation unsatisfactory. Their discoveries were not altogether new, as if they arrived all at once at the conclusions they drew.

John Wycliffe (1329–1384) had emphasized the sufficiency and final authority of Holy Scripture over 100 years *before* Luther. And like Luther, he had raised his voice against the church's opulence and the sale of indulgences. John Huss (1373–1415) had sought to define the church more consistently by Christlike living rather than by the administration of the sacraments. He also emphasized the authority of Scripture and opposed the sale of indulgences, as well as the veneration of images. John of Wessel (1420–1489), a German theologian, had denied transubstantiation, opposed the sale of indulgences, and rejected priestly celibacy. Girolamo Savonarola (1452–1498), an Italian Dominican monk, had been hanged and burned for heresy in Florence because he had preached powerfully against papal immorality just a few decades before Luther's protest.

In light of the clear message of Scripture, many leaders, and even some common folk, had come to peace with God. They had a full assurance of faith, a rare thing in those times. And many saw serious problems within the church, though not all would take action, which might well lead to death as a heretic. Modern readers must not fail to appreciate just how profound a challenge Luther had made. Let me elaborate briefly.

Throughout the Middle Ages many reformations had occurred within the life of the church. But none drove such a deep chasm as this. These earlier movements were primarily interested in moral reform. Abuses of institutional and personal life were often addressed. The Protestant Reformation began as another reforming movement for the moral life of the church. But the essence of its thrust became, within two to three years, *radically* doctrinal. Even by 1520, less than three years after Luther had challenged the abusive sale of indulgences, he focused his concerns primarily on important doctrinal issues in two of his most important tracts: *The Babylonian Captivity of the Church* and *The Appeal to the German Nobility.*

Philip Melanchthon, a friend of Luther's, summarized the Protestant concerns in the Augsburg Confession (1530), stating very positively the Protestant position regarding the important theological issues at stake. John Calvin, a second-generation Protestant Reformer, argued more clearly for a complete reformation of the church in his classic work *The Institutes of the Christian Religion.* This became the most significant systematic theology of the entire evangelical cause.

But why did the evangelicals of the sixteenth century feel compelled to move outside the Roman Church? It was not a rash decision on their part. According to the accepted theology of their time, they were cutting themselves off from the grace of God, an act that could potentially destroy them spiritually. This was their birth church. It was the church that had nursed their immortal souls. It was the visible communion of faith. What would make them leave—and at such great sacrifice? Historian Robert Godfrey answers this question:

> Historians . . . have given attention to the political, social, and economic circumstances of the sixteenth century to understand the setting of the Reformation. They have studied the cultural and intellectual developments of the late medieval and Renaissance periods as crucial backdrop for the Reformation. But ultimately it was not these factors that divided the church. These factors may have contributed in a variety of ways to the success of the Reformation, but they were not the heart of the Reformation. The heart of the Reformation was *a distinct spiritual and theological vision*—quite different from the one that had dominated the medieval church (emphasis added).[1]

The Line in the Sand

The defining issues of the evangelical movement are not difficult to determine. Nor are they too numerous to be simply observed. As theologians wrote and preached, important issues surfaced. It was not long before the genuinely significant matters were plainly stated and the lines drawn that determined the direction of both parties.

Today, some people respond, "Of course Luther was right. The church had made some big mistakes, and it still does. But that doesn't make the whole Roman Catholic system wrong, does it?" In a system as all-encompassing as that of the Roman Church, an attack upon any of its well-entrenched practices was understood as an attack upon the whole church itself. This was the medieval way of thinking. Only in a postmodern pluralistic age like our own, where hardly any single truth is consistently confessed or carefully connected to other truths, do we think otherwise.

When Luther asked, "What is an indulgence and of what value is it?" this led logically to a full discussion of the sacrament of penance. This challenge, as we saw in the last chapter, called into question the Roman Catholic doctrine of salvation. His questions, "Can the pope grant an indulgence and what kind of indulgence can he grant?" led immediately to the more profound question, "What is the nature of papal authority?" And these questions led back to the ultimate challenge: "What is the church?"

The course the Reformation took in its early days followed this line of reasoning consistently. Luther was urged to silence while the church prepared a reply to his challenges. In 1518 he met at Augsburg with a papal delegation, and it was here that Cardinal Cajetan demanded that Luther recant his statement. Luther said that he could not recant unless his writings were shown to be false by the plain teaching of Scripture. A short truce followed, but in 1519 Luther was publicly attacked by

Eck, the papal theologian. Luther was asked to support Eck's traditional view that divine power was inherent in the papacy. Luther refused, saying that the pope's power was of human right, not divine. To support this he developed an important thesis that he drew from earlier theologians such as Augustine: *The church is in reality a spiritual fellowship of all those who truly believe in Christ.* It was here that Luther demonstrated that popes and councils had erred. It struck a blow that rocked the medieval system at its foundation.

After Luther was denounced by Eck, he was threatened with excommunication by the church. His writings were condemned as "heretical, erroneous, or offensive to pious ears." His writings were to be found, wherever possible, and publicly burned. In response, on December 10, 1520, Luther publicly burned a copy of the document of excommunication (called a "bull") in front of the entire student body of the University of Wittenberg. His actual excommunication followed on January 2, 1521. Even before this, Luther had already voluntarily left the church, declaring that the pope was "antichrist" and that Rome had become a "nest of the devil."

The Turning Point

By this time, Luther had reached the place where there was no turning back. The line had been drawn. But why? What was the turning point for this previously devout and loyal monk?

The Leipzig debate with Eck in the summer of 1519 had emboldened Luther considerably. He had come to see that his growing disagreement with the papal church was not simply a matter of indulgences and moral abuses. In tract after tract, written in Latin for scholars and in German for the people, he attacked the teachings of the medieval church that he believed undermined the two principle concerns that drove him—the authority of the believer and the church, *and* the nature of grace and faith as they relate to salvation.

Luther's understanding of certain doctrines grew as he studied the Bible more carefully. Some of his views probably never matured as they might have if he had listened to other Reformers more carefully. He was a singularly courageous and bold man, often given to strong statements and radical actions. His language is notoriously rough and coarse at times, but this belonged to the spirit of his age. He was just the man needed for the time. His style, wrote one historian, was "bold, rugged, picturesque and wonderfully clear." His words were those spoken by the average German. His writings, therefore, were in eager demand. Even in France and England, where his works were published in Latin, people read Luther.

But what teachings brought about the irreconcilable division that remains with us nearly 500 years later? There are many in our day who say that perhaps, after all this time, we have changed sufficiently in our understanding of these vital doctrines that now we can openly heal the breach brought about by this so-called "wild boar" of the German vineyard. Perhaps we can forge a "common mission" in this age of secular humanism if our differences are no longer as large as they were in Luther's time, so goes the reasoning.

Two Vital Truths

As previously noted, Luther and the Protestant evangelicals believed that two important truths stood at the heart of their reforming effort. Modern readers need to understand why these two truths are vital to the life of the church.

These two issues are still central to the theological differences between evangelicals and Roman Catholics today. They are what we call the *formal* and *material* principles of the Reformation. It is imperative that we understand these two vital truths, for, if Rome is correct on these points, then the Protestant Reformers were wrong. But if the Protestant Reformers got it right, then the Reformation is certainly *not* over, and talk of formal agreement at the core of our beliefs cannot succeed.

The Formal Principle of the Reformation

We call it the formal principle because it is the thing that forms and shapes. It determines what Christians believe and why. The popular catchphrase for this principle is "Scripture alone." What that means is that the church cannot preach, teach, command, or practice anything contrary to Scripture, even for very good and necessary reasons. The church's authority is not inherently in itself but is rather derived from the written Scriptures alone. The church's task is actually quite simple—pass along to the faithful what the Scriptures teach, and nothing else!

It is necessary that we understand what the evangelicals did *not* mean by this principle. First, individuals are *not* free to decide for themselves what to believe. They are obligated to the Scriptures. They cannot, willy-nilly, pick and choose their authority. Further, this principle did *not* mean that each individual Christian could interpret the Bible as he or she pleased, in opposition to the consensus of the church and its concerns over the centuries. Luther, in typically blunt fashion, wrote, "Each man could go to hell in his own way." By this he meant, in essence, "Go ahead and fashion your own *private* doctrines from the text. Realize, however, that such may well condemn you if you conclude falsely regarding the doctrines of Christ and salvation, the central and clear concern of all Holy Scripture."

The Reformers were careful to demonstrate that what they taught was not something discovered in the sixteenth century. They sought to show how their teachings were in harmony with the Fathers of the early church, especially the great theologian Augustine. They believed that they were rediscovering something very old—lost by a corrupt Rome. Though *complete* agreement with the church's consensus was not required for every doctrine, all teaching was to be submitted in humility to the communion of the saints with a clear demonstration that this was in fact the teaching of the Bible.

Although it is true that different Protestant communions came to differing conclusions on some important matters, such as the nature of communion and baptism, it is *not* true that they differed in the *fundamental* principles of the Reformation. They were in unanimous agreement when they challenged the claim that tradition was a source of revelation alongside the written Scriptures. They were unanimous in their opposition when Rome claimed that teaching authority lay in the magisterium (the teaching office of the Catholic Church), with the pope as its chief shepherd under Christ. Against the Catholic claim of continued revelation through the church the Reformers pressed the truth of the sufficiency of Scripture.

But, said the Catholic apologists, even with an infallible and sufficient Bible, you still don't have an infallible teacher. The Protestant Reformers answered this objection by using the arguments of Catholic humanists such as Erasmus to show how popes and councils in the Middle Ages had made contradictory claims. As Michael Horton has said,

> The best way to guard a true interpretation of Scripture, the Reformers insisted, was neither to naively embrace the infallibility of tradition, nor the infallibility of the individual, but to recognize the *communal* interpretation of Scripture. The best way to ensure faithfulness to the text is to read it together, not only with the churches of our own time and place, but with the wider "communion of saints" down through the ages.[2]

The community of a church might err, but there will always be much wisdom in many counselors (see Proverbs 11:14). We are most likely to get the meaning of Scripture right when we come to it believing that the text is infallible and we are not!

But what is the message of the Bible? Granting its infallibility and final authority for faith and practice we must ask, What does the Bible teach? Put very plainly, How am I saved and reconciled to God? Surely this is *the* question that we must answer if we are to know and serve Christ.

The Material Principle of the Reformation

The longing of every devout person who lived before Christ came to earth was expressed in the question, "How can I know God?" Israel's hope and consolation was in the promise of a coming deliverer, a Messiah. Her temple services, sacrificial system, carefully developed priesthood, unusual prophets, and royal kings all pointed to something or someone superior to all the shadows and types of the ritualistic system. All Christians agree that this person was Jesus Christ. Here is the "desire of every nation," as one hymn writer put it.

But how am I made right with God in Jesus Christ? How do I know that I have come into the salvation that He brings? Very simply, "Sirs, what must I do to be saved?" (Acts 16:30). Note the answer given by the apostle Paul: "Believe in the Lord Jesus, and you will be saved—you and your household" (verse 31). Paul says the same thing in unmistakably clear language in Romans: "To the man who does not work but trusts God who justifies the wicked, his faith is credited as righteousness" (4:5).

The Reformers referred to this doctrine of justification as "the article by which the church stands or falls." By this they did not mean a person was saved by virtue of understanding the full ramifications of this great truth. Rather, he or she was saved by faith in Christ alone, and that through grace alone. But here the visible church must stand on Christ alone as the sole basis for justification before a holy God, or it will fall. A person who *truly* trusts Christ alone will be saved, whether or not he or she fully understands this article. (Who can fully understand any article of truth?)

The Reformers never tired of insisting that justification was a legal (forensic) concept. The term *justification* was the term of a law court. It was a word that described a change in status. It was the opposite of "guilty" or "condemned." To be justified was, very simply, to be right with God. Nothing could be added to this status and nothing subtracted.

The Reformers often spoke of justification as resting entirely upon the merits of Jesus Christ alone. We rest, they argued, upon the obedience of Christ, which is imputed to us on the basis of our faith in Him alone. We do not grow into this grace or find favor with God over time as we experience the impartation of new life to our souls. We are immediately accepted by God, fully and finally, on the basis of Christ and His work for us.

Rome's argument was, and still is (formally), that Christ's righteousness is infused into the believer's heart, wherein a process begins that leads to final justification. Jerome, who produced the Latin Vulgate translation of the Bible, actually translated the Greek word that meant "to *declare* righteous" as "to *make* righteous." When Greek scholars challenged this in the pre-Reformation era, in effect, it pried open the door for a better understanding of Scripture itself. When Luther came to see this truth, he said, "It was as if the windows of heaven were flung open and I was born again." So he was.

Summing Up

The Reformers believed that the Church of Rome had abandoned these two vital principles. The first principle they saw in Scripture and the church fathers. The second, though not as plainly developed in the writings of the early church, they saw in budlike form in Augustine's teaching, especially with regard to the sovereignty of grace in salvation and the priority of God's will in granting faith to those who believe. They insisted that on both counts the Scriptures agreed with them and that doctrinal reform based on the plain teaching of the Word of God was desperately needed. This meant that the teachings and practices that had developed in the late Middle Ages had to go. True reform was necessary, even at the expense of visible unity in the church.

How did Rome respond to this serious challenge? To that we now turn our attention.

CHAPTER FOUR

A Fallen Church?

If the evangelical Reformers' views were correct, Rome was a *falling* church in the era immediately prior to the Protestant Reformation. She had substantially departed from the authority and sufficiency of Scripture. Centuries of extra-biblical tradition, as well as the development of nonapostolic practices, had led her progressively away from the simplicity of New Testament Christianity (for example, sacramentalism—the belief that grace is conveyed through rites of the church, the veneration of Mary and the saints, the doctrine of purgatory, and so on. These particular beliefs and practices will be examined in chapters 5–9). More significantly, she had departed from the gospel of grace, though her theologians continually tried to demonstrate otherwise. How did the church *officially* reply to the charges that she had departed from both Scripture and the gospel?

Let's be very clear about this. These were extremely serious charges the Reformers made. We are not considering minor issues that churches will sometimes dispute for no good purpose. The apostle Paul wrote to the Galatian church that "even if we or an angel from heaven should preach to you a gospel other than the one we preached to you, let him be eternally condemned!" (Galatians 1:8). The same apostle said that "Satan himself masquerades as an angel of light" (2 Corinthians 11:14), thus warning believers to be careful that the gospel they embrace is consistent with the content of the gospel as preached by the apostles themselves. Innovations may be useful, but there is no room for innovation in the message of the evangel.

By 1520, only three short years after Luther had nailed his famous *Ninety-five Theses* to the university church door in Wittenberg, he had become the best-known man in all of Germany. His following came from several circles within the larger society. All who opposed the church for any reason applauded him because of his boldness in attacking the Catholic Church. Scholars saw in him a man who could help break the chains of intellectual oppression in the universities. German nationalists saw in him a leader pointing the way to political liberty. The peasants rallied to him as a deliverer who would help them find economic freedom. Sadly, only a few saw his real concern—the theological reformation of the church. Some who did understand were Nicholas Amsdorf, John Brenz, and Philip Melanchthon. These individuals, with various nonscholars here and there, were drawn to Luther's writings and preaching because of his clear insights regarding the gospel.

As we saw briefly in chapter 3, Luther's primary concern was centered on the gospel message of justification by faith alone. This was not a novel idea; it was the teaching of Romans 4:5 and Galatians 3:22. It had never disappeared entirely from the historic church, but Luther was to give it new meaning by making it the primary article of the church—*the defining principle* of the Christian life. Here faith could grow, assurance would be solidified, and the saints could flourish in faith and hope.

In Luther's theological emphasis, *justification* is seen as a definitive act of God. It is a grace given to sinners for the sake of Christ, whereby He forgives people all their sin and counts them entirely righteous. He grants this pardon on the basis of their receiving the free gift of eternal life in Christ alone. Justification must not be confused with sanctification, an act wherein a process begins and continues. In *sanctification,* which is always present when a person is justified, God makes people progressively more holy. Thus, a person can be fully justified, yet partially sanctified. This, indeed, is always the case, because even the godliest people are, as Luther put it, simultaneously sinful yet completely justified.

But here is the critical point: In justification, there is no room for growth. There is no partial, progressive, or continuing justification going on inside the life of a believer in Christ. A person is either entirely justified or he is not. And justification comes to sinful people on the basis of God's kindness and goodness alone. It is a gift God bestows, not a status a person achieves. The word *merit* can, therefore, have absolutely no place in this matter. This insight struck at the very heart of what had developed during the Middle Ages (see chapter 2).

God is holy. He cannot allow sinful creatures into fellowship with Himself. All the confession in the world cannot make a sinner anything other than a sinner. Luther understood this. His deep preoccupation with his own sin had almost driven him insane. Because of this, countless psychotherapeutic writers have attacked him as a neurotic and semideranged person. What he was, in the best medieval sense, was a man who believed explicitly in the teaching of his church regarding the fear of God, His awesome power, and His determination to judge sin.

What Luther came to understand in 1517 and beyond was that God is also gracious. He had provided satisfaction for mankind's offense against Himself in the death of Christ. Here salvation is freely provided. In the gospel an announcement is given and an offer is made. This is grace—not some magical power that pours grace into hearts through the mystery of sacraments. God grants grace to sinners, but they must accept it. This is faith—trusting in God for Christ's sake, or, simply put, entrusting all that I am as a sinner to all that Christ is as a Savior.

This is not bare acknowledgment or creedal affirmation. It is leaning oneself entirely upon the person and work of Jesus as offered in the gospel. Faith is relationship—trust by me, a single person, in Christ, another person, who redeems me by His life and death. It is all based solely on the grace of God. When I believe the gospel, I am counted (credited, reckoned) as righteous immediately. And God gives me His Spirit, through whom I am empowered to begin, for the first time, to do works that God finds acceptable because of Christ.

A New Authority?

For this faith to be born in people, the promises of God are essential. These promises are the gospel of grace. They come through the Scriptures, especially as they are properly preached. For Luther all of Scripture consisted of law and gospel. Both are the Word of God. Through the law people come to know the will of God and His stern, righteous, holy demands. From the same Scriptures people learn of the gospel, the free grace of a benevolent God who will forgive.

The Scriptures are God's Word because here He speaks. They are given by the inspiration of the Holy Spirit (literally, "breathed out by the Spirit"). This means that the resulting text of the written word is exactly and infallibly what God intended. The personalities of human authors can be seen in the written Scriptures, but the result of their writing is God's Word!

What Luther claimed for the Scriptures is still important today. He believed that God continued to speak to men and women, but only through the Scriptures. Indeed, only through

Scripture does God come to people with His truth and clearly reveal Himself. He does not reveal Himself infallibly through church organizations, special mystical revelations, ecstatic visions, or apparitions. The only *authority* the visible church truly has is that of the Scriptures. If the church departs from the Word of God, it is a blind guide and will fall into the ditch, taking many others with it. Further, the Scriptures will not yield correct interpretation except to a person of faith. Rationalistic, humanistic wisdom will serve no salvific purpose when it comes to handling the Scriptures.

When the Scriptures come to a person as a sinner, they rouse his sleeping conscience via the law and its demands. He is convicted of sin, righteousness, and judgment to come, as Jesus taught. He then must flee to the promises of the gospel. The law cannot help him one iota. When the sinner has believed the gospel, he then sees the law in a new way, as a guide for his conduct because of the grace revealed in the gospel. The law will never conquer sin within the believer, but it will repeatedly inform him regarding proper thought and conduct, and it will drive him back to the gospel day after day. Here alone he will find safety.

But What About the Church?

From this it stands to reason that the church cannot be the institution that mediates salvation to the souls of people through the mystery of its operations. The church is to be understood, primarily, as a "communion of saints," or a spiritual fellowship of all who believe the gospel and are justified. What the visible church can and must do is bring men and women to the Word of God. It does this in two ways—preaching and the sacraments. The gospel is presented in word through preaching, and it is presented by divine symbol through the sacraments.

In its preaching the church should declare both the law and the gospel. In the sacraments (literally, "sacred signs") it declares God's promises with the signs given to her by Christ. Protestant Reformers disagreed among themselves regarding the *nature* of these signs, but all agreed that there were only two clearly delineated in the Scriptures (baptism and holy communion, or the Lord's Supper). Rome believed, and still teaches, that there are seven sacraments. (In addition to baptism and communion, Rome adds these: confirmation, penance, anointing the sick, holy orders, and marriage. We will look at these in chapter 6.)

The evangelical Reformers believed that the Word was effective. Wherever it was preached in faith it would have a powerful effect—namely in bringing God's elect to eternal life. And where this Word gathers a people who believe the gospel, you have a visible church after the pattern of the New Testament. This means that the church does not need a continuation of bishops or a constant ecclesiastical government to form an organized body truly faithful to the New Testament. Indeed, the church is free under the Word of God to organize itself as an assembly of believers with gospel ministers. Those believers who form such a church are free to set up or depose teachers in accordance with guidelines found in God's Word.

These are essentially the great truths recovered and plainly taught by the Protestants of the sixteenth century. Their consistent application breaks down the Roman synthesis of the Middle Ages; these principles attack the very foundation of the papacy, the magisterium (the official teaching authority of the church), and the sacramental system of Rome. But why?

The grace of God cannot be mediated by the church through her rule over the souls of people and, at the same time, by the Word of God alone. If the disputants of the sixteenth century were anything, and this was true on both sides, they were logically consistent. They both believed in the law of noncontradiction. This means that two mutually exclusive claims cannot both be true at the same time. Both might be wrong, but if one is correct the other must be wrong.

Luther's approach also attacked the apparatus of ritualism. It set up the preaching of God's Word and the proper administration of the two warranted sacraments as the sole function of the church. (Calvin later added, upon further biblical reflection, the so-called "third mark" of the visible church-discipline.)

Luther and the Reformers were not radicals in how they viewed history. They believed that however corrupt the church had become it had reached this low point under God's sovereign purpose. God had permitted this course for a purpose, even if it was to punish sin in the leaders. What history has revealed should not be discarded lightly and flippantly. If what we see around us is contrary to the revealed will of God, then it must be abolished, but totally tearing down the church was never the Reformers' desire. They worked to retain all that they could as well as to conserve the heritage of the past. They frequently appealed to the writings of the church fathers. They read and understood the theologians of the Middle Ages. This was especially true for Luther. But what kept the Catholic Church from embracing the theological distinctives of the Reformation?

The Counter-Reformation and the Council of Trent

In 1523, Rome sought to correct its abuses in the whole matter of indulgences and immoral practice in the priesthood by launching a reformation movement of its own. Pope Hadrian VI acknowledged that the church needed a thorough reformation, which would begin at Rome itself. Unfortunately Hadrian died before he could begin this effort, and his successor, Clement VII (1523–1534), was chosen partly on his expressed *opposition* to this reforming effort.

During the next ten years efforts to reform the church continued from within. New societies of priests were formed, as had been the case during previous centuries. Charles V pressed the church for a general council to discuss theological matters. In 1536 those who were calling for change and those who were opposed to change formed a consensus that resulted in changes both at Rome itself and later in the church at large. Pope Pius III appointed to the college of cardinals "reform-minded" men, and from their number eventually came three reforming popes in the decades that followed.

During this time the call for a general papal council grew stronger and stronger. This council finally convened in 1545, just months before Luther's death in February of 1546. The council met in the northern part of Italy at the city of Trent on three different occasions, finally finishing its work in 1563. (This is considered, by the Catholic Church, to be the nineteenth general council in church history.) The Council of Trent had three purposes in its meetings, all of which are stated in a papal bull (document). First, the council sought to define Catholic doctrine more clearly, especially as over against the doctrine of the Protestant evangelicals. Second, it worked toward reforming church life. Third, it purposed to clarify present heresies and drive them out of the church of Rome completely.

The doctrines adopted by this historic council were essentially restatements of the doctrinal positions of the later Middle Ages. These were the very teachings that the Protestant Reformers had struggled against. The council clearly had the writings of Luther and Calvin in mind, if not actually in hand, and what was written strongly repudiated the essential doctrinal tenets of the evangelical Reformers.

The decrees relating to church reform also dealt with matters raised by the Protestants. They urged greater pastoral care for the laity and more effective preaching by priests. The whole oversight of the bishops over dioceses was strengthened in a practical sense. Some decrees of the council addressed the need for real reformation in papal practices, but the council was not unified on this matter. The question of the pope's supremacy over the whole church—which was and still is a stumbling block for many—was also treated, but no clear decision was reached.

As the council met between 1545 and 1563, there was a glimmer of hope that the Roman Church would come to openly embrace the light of the gospel of grace that had broken out across Europe. Some cardinals in the church saw truth in the concerns of the Reformers. The rejection of the gospel by the pope was not yet solidified in these days. Michael Horton correctly sums up the situation:

> The door was open to the full reformation of Western Christendom until the Council of Trent . . . finally closed it with its devastating canons against the gospel. Things that had been left to debate in the universities were now closed to discussion as the council issued what it considered infallible pronouncements on the doctrine of justification and related truths. Now, issues upon which men and women of goodwill could differ were given a single answer: tradition is equal to Scripture in authority; the interpretation of Scripture and the elements of Holy Communion are to be denied to the laity; the Mass is a repetition of Christ's sacrifice and each Mass atones for the people; transubstantiation was officially affirmed, as was belief in purgatory.[1]

What was sad about this is that it left the church deeply divided. What was sadder still was the longest decree of this council—the one titled "Concerning Justification." The beginning portions of this decree are agreeable to both Reformers and Catholics. They attack the major errors cited by Augustine against Pelagius in the early controversies of the church. But within this portion comes this line: "they who by sin had been cut off from God may be disposed through His quickening and helping grace to convert themselves to their own justification by freely assenting to and cooperating with that grace." A person cannot, said the document, "by his own free will and without the grace of God" move himself toward justice in the sight of God, yet he can and must *cooperate* with grace in the end.

What follows is a definition that is crucial to understanding the present great divide. The council defined justification as "not only a remission of sins but also the sanctification and renewal of the inward man through the voluntary reception of grace and gifts whereby an unjust man becomes just." This is in clear contradiction to Luther's teaching and other Protestants who insisted, with the apostle Paul, that justification and sanctification are not one and the same. Sanctification should not be denied, but the renewal of the inward believer is not the same thing as justification. *Justification is a once-and-for-all act. Sanctification is an ongoing process.*

In justification we move immediately, on the basis of faith alone, from being unjust, condemned, lost, and without hope into a position of being just, acquitted, saved, and filled with true hope! In contrast to this, the Council of Trent said that God puts His Spirit within us in order to renew us and move us progressively from being unjust to being just. This is a *process*, albeit one begun and ostensibly carried out by grace, but nonetheless a process. But this is not what is taught in Romans 4:1-5, where Paul said that justification comes to those who are wicked, who stop trying to work for it, and who therefore accept it by faith alone. Paul's clear point is this: God justifies the sinner *as a sinner,* not on the basis of anything done in the flesh. This is the good news—the gospel!

Let's consider the differences between the two views by way of the following four-point contrast that lists the Catholic and Reformation doctrines of justification:

Roman Catholic Doctrine	Reformation Doctrine
1. Justified by God's work of grace *in* a person	1. Justified by God's work of grace *in* Christ
2. Justified by faith, which has become active by *charity* (true love)	2. Justified by faith *alone*
3. Justified by *infused* righteousness	3. Justified by *imputed* righteousness
4. Justification means *making* righteous *in one's own person*	4. Justification means that a person is *accounted as righteous*

If all of this seems to be an overstatement of the differences between the Reformers' understanding of justification and that of the Catholic Church, consider the strong language of several canons of the decree on justification from the Council of Trent:

> *Canon 9.* If anyone says that the sinner is justified by faith Alone . . . , meaning that nothing else is required to cooperate in order to obtain the grace of justification, and that it is not in any way necessary that he be prepared and disposed by the action of his own will, let him be anathema.
>
> *Canon 11.* If anyone says that men are justified either by the sole imputation of the justice of Christ or by the sole remission of sins, to the exclusion of the grace and charity which is poured forth in their hearts by the Holy Ghost (Romans 5:5), and remains in them, or also that the grace by which we are justified is only the good will of God, let him be anathema.
>
> *Canon 12.* If anyone says that justifying faith is nothing else than confidence in divine mercy . . . which remits sins for Christ's sake, or that it is this confidence alone that justifies us, let him be anathema.
>
> *Canon 24.* If anyone says that the justice received is not preserved and also not increased before God through good

> works... but that those works are merely the fruits and signs of justification obtained, but not the cause of the increase, let him be anathema.
>
> *Canon 30.* If anyone says that after the reception of the grace of justification the guilt is so remitted and the debt of eternal punishment so blotted out to every repentant sinner, that no debt of temporal punishment remains to be discharged either in this world or in purgatory before the gates of heaven can be opened, let him be anathema.
>
> *Canon 32.* If anyone says that the good works of the one justified are in such manner the gifts of God that they are not also the good merits of him justified; or that the one justified by the good works that he performs by the grace of God and the merit of Jesus Christ, whose living member he is, does not truly merit an increase of grace, eternal life, and in case he dies in grace the attainment of eternal life itself and also an increase of glory, let him be anathema.

Summing Up

What all this plainly affirmed, according to the Council of Trent, is that sinners are made right with God over the course of their entire lives (and beyond) on the basis of their cooperating with God's grace. They cooperate with God through the inner work of the Holy Spirit rather than on the basis of faith in the finished work of Christ on the cross. Surely there is no room for any remaining doubt when we conclude, in the spirit of gentleness, that the answer given to the vital question, "What must I do to be saved?" has two radically different answers. One answer was confessed by the Reformers (and by evangelicals since), while the other was confessed by the Council of Trent (and the Catholic Church since). The evangelical answer says the only thing you can and must do is "believe." The Catholic mystery says, just as plainly, that you must believe but you must also continue on in the way of sacramental mystery in and through the church. These answers, plainly, are *radically* different.

What happened at Trent may not be irreversible. God alone knows. Present Catholic biblical scholarship has increasingly understood the New Testament in ways that are fresh and vital. This has brought about a measure of renewed discussion about some of the same important matters passionately debated in the sixteenth century. However, it is clear that no Catholic council or creed since Trent has fundamentally *altered* either the language or the theology of this important sixteenth-century decision. Historically, evangelicals have believed that a door was closed by this particular council—a door that many of us pray might someday be reopened.

We shall return to this matter of the church later on. For now it is important that evangelical readers understand the real difficulties this issue raises for their friends who are devout Catholics. One former Catholic puts this difficulty into proper perspective by stating how hard it was to repeatedly face the question that ached within his soul: "Did I really leave the Holy Catholic Church?" Evangelicals do not relate well to this type of question, since for most of them the church is only a voluntary society they can leave at will. However, for the devout Catholic this question is both daunting and disturbing. After all, he was baptized into this communion by loving parents and God-fearing people. How can one leave home, the very place where Christ has been known since childhood?

Another friend, who eventually chose to leave Catholicism after a long struggle, notes that "this may be the question either you or someone you know is pondering. My search for peace ended, ultimately, by finding the answer to a similar question: 'Is the Roman Catholic Church a fallen church?' The answer, I came to realize, lies in what constitutes a fallen church." This individual's answer sums up the point of this chapter. He concludes: "Seeing as how the chief treasure of the true church is the gospel of Jesus Christ, and how the chief mandate given to that church is the great commission, then the entire matter, for me, was finally resolved when I more carefully studied Rome's gospel."

Therefore, we now turn to a consideration of the primary reasons why evangelicals and Catholics do *not* have the same understanding of the gospel. This is, after all, the nub of why we must continue our dialogue while maintaining a profound concern for the teaching of Scripture itself. We do agree, as we have already seen, on much that is important. Recent decades have seen us discuss the gospel and the meaning of Christ's life and death as never before. This is even truer in our present cultural context. But we still do *not* agree on the gospel itself. This issue cannot be buried under a sea of good will, not so long as men and women think, study their Bibles, and truly care about the most vital of all questions: "What must I do to be saved?" The differences in the respective answers offered by confessional Catholicism and biblically informed evangelicalism are substantive, and they are still vital.

Are You Catholic or Evangelical?

The following is a quiz designed to underscore the *essential* differences between Catholic and evangelical understandings of the doctrine of justification by faith, which, as we have seen already and will see again and again throughout this book, was one of the two central theological debates in the sixteenth century.

In each of the ten choices below choose either (a) or (b). The answers are in the back of the book, on page 214. Take the quiz now and save a list of your answers. Then see if you better understand the correct answers *after* you have read all of *The Catholic Mystery*.

1. (a) God gives a person right standing with Himself by mercifully accounting him innocent and virtuous.

   (b) God gives a person right standing with Himself by actually making him into an innocent and virtuous person.

2. (a) God gives a person right standing with Himself by placing Christ's goodness and virtue to his credit.

   (b) God gives a person right standing with Himself by putting Christ's goodness and virtue into his heart.

3. (a) God accepts the believer because of the moral excellence found in Jesus Christ.

   (b) God makes the believer acceptable by infusing Christ's moral excellence into his life.

4. (a) If a Christian becomes "born again" (regenerate, transformed in character), he will achieve right standing with God.

   (b) If the sinner accepts right standing with God by faith, he will then experience transformation in character.

5. (a) We receive right standing with God by faith alone.

   (b) We receive right standing with God by faith that has become active by (through) love.

6. (a) We achieve right standing with God by having Christ live out His life of obedience in us.

   (b) We achieve right standing with God by accepting the fact that He obeyed the law perfectly for us.

7. (a) We achieve right standing with God by following Christ's example through the help of His enabling grace.

   (b) We follow Christ's example because His life has already given us right standing with God.

8. (a) God first pronounces (declares) that we are good in His sight, then gives us His Spirit to make us good.

   (b) God sends His Spirit to make us good, and then He will pronounce (declare) that we are good.

9. (a) Christ's intercession at God's right hand gives us favor in God's sight.

   (b) It is the indwelling Christ in our heart that gives us favor in God's sight.

10. (a) Only by faith in the doing and dying of Christ can we fully satisfy the requirements of the Ten Commandments.

    (b) By the power of the Holy Spirit living in us, we can fully satisfy the requirements of the Ten Commandments.

PART 2

The Theological Issues

The Protestant Reformation originally set out to address several abuses in the church, especially regarding the sale of indugences. Before three years had passed deeper issues surfaced in the midst of a major debate. These issues were not to be easily corrected through the moral and social changes initiated by Rome.

By the 1520s the central issues of the debate revolved around two major doctrinal points. These two points were known as the formal and material principles of the Reformation. The formal principle, that which formed the Reformation, was the doctrine of Scripture. What is authority? And where is it found? In the church, or in the Bible alone? Is the written Scripture sufficient for all faith and practice? What is the place of tradition, of the teaching authority of the pope and the church? How should we respond to councils, creeds, and confessions if they conflict with the written Word? Is the central teaching of Scripture clear?

The material principle was equally important. In this the Protestant Reformers followed Paul's teaching in Romans that people are made right with God by Christ alone through grace alone. The key part of this equation was that Christ and grace were received by faith alone. By this the Reformers stressed that true faith laid hold of Christ and the grace of God without any human merit.

These two principles exposed a number of serious theological differences with Rome that are still the cause of division today.

CHAPTER FIVE

The Central Mystery of the Christian Faith?

Dr. Scott Hahn, formerly an evangelical minister, recently told the story of his conversion to Roman Catholicism in a popularly written account entitled *Rome Sweet Home.* Scott, an engaging apologist for the Catholic faith, describes the final stage of his journey in terms of his finally receiving the Mass. He writes:

> After pronouncing the words of consecration, the priest held up the Host. I felt as if the last drop of doubt had drained from me. With all my heart, I whispered, "My Lord and my God. That's really you! And if that's you, then I want full communion with you. I don't want to hold anything back." ... Day after day, witnessing the entire drama of the Mass I saw the covenant renewed right before my eyes. I knew Christ wanted me to receive him in faith, not just spiritually in my heart, but physically as well: onto my tongue, down in my throat and into my whole body and soul. This was what the Incarnation was all about. This was the gospel in its fullness.[1]

When Scott Hahn finally made the decision to openly become a Roman Catholic he describes his struggle with God in a simple, straightforward way:

> So I went to the Lord in prayer. "Lord, what do you want *me* to do?" I remember praying that and thinking, I wonder why I haven't asked you that before now? "Lord, what do you want me to do?"
>
> I was utterly taken aback when, to my surprise, I felt his response back to me, "What is it, my son, that *you* want to do?"
>
> That was easy. I didn't have to think twice. "Father, I want to come home. I want to receive you, Jesus, my eldest Brother and Lord, in the Holy Eucharist."[2]

What Hahn describes in the above account every devoted cradle Catholic, or new convert, understands. And every true Catholic who knows something of the church's doctrine understands exactly why Scott Hahn says he wanted to "receive" Jesus "in the Holy Eucharist" and thus enter into the Catholic mystery. These sentiments express the view and longing of every faithful Catholic. This accords, plainly, with what the church actually teaches.

Most evangelical Christians have no understanding of statements such as these, especially if they have grown up thinking that the Lord's Supper is just a memorial celebrated at the beginning or end of an otherwise ordinary worship service. One thing is for sure: Most evangelicals have little or no place for mystery. But not so with Catholic worship, which centers on the mystery of Christ and His redemptive work.

For centuries the central mystery and feature of Roman Catholic worship and practice has clearly been the Mass. Most Catholics know more about the Mass than almost any other aspect of their faith. This, quite simply, is the heart and soul of Catholic life and faith. Few evangelicals understand Catholic dogma at this point. What exactly is the Mass? What happens in the Mass, according to Catholic teaching? Where and how did this practice actually begin? And, most importantly, what does the New Testament say about the Lord's Supper as instituted by Christ on the night He was betrayed?

The Roman Catholic Doctrine of the Mass

When you talk to any three or four Catholics, you will hear various views of the Mass. The same can be said of evangelicals. Ask any three or four of them what happens in their church when the Lord's Supper, or communion, is taken, and the answers will vary widely. Confusion abounds in our respective groups. It is best, therefore, that we not get a definition of the Mass from the "street" but from official sources and statements. It is important that evangelicals not misrepresent Catholic doctrine regarding the Mass.

For years a standard catechism used by Catholic teachers for training communicants was the book titled *A Catechism of Christian Doctrine*. It says, "The Holy Mass is one and the same with that of the Cross, inasmuch as Christ, who offered Himself, a bleeding victim, on the Cross to His Heavenly father, continues to offer Himself in an unbloody manner on the altar, through the ministry of His priests."[3] This definition is quite consistent with the older Catholic teaching set forth in the doctrine of the Council of Trent (1545–1563). There isn't much room for misunderstanding the doctrine's implications when the words of the "Canons on the Sacrifice of the Mass" are read carefully:

> *Canon 1.* If anyone says that in the mass a true and real sacrifice is not offered to God; or that to be offered is nothing else than that Christ is given to us to eat, let him be anathema.
>
> *Canon 2.* If anyone says by those words "Do this for a commemoration of me," Christ did not institute the apostles

> priests, or did not ordain that they and other priests should offer his own body and blood, let him be anathema.
>
> *Canon 3.* If anyone says that the sacrifice of the mass is only a sacrifice of praise and thanksgiving; or that it is a bare commemoration of the sacrifice consummated on the cross but not a propitiatory sacrifice...let him be anathema.

The title of chapter 2 of the "Doctrine Concerning the Sacrifice of the Mass" (from the twenty-second session, September 17, 1562) is "The Sacrifice of the Mass Is Propitiatory Both for the Living and the Dead." This section says,

> And inasmuch as this divine sacrifice which is celebrated in the Mass is contained and immolated [offered] in an unbloody manner the same Christ who once offered Himself in a bloody manner on the altar of the cross, the holy council teaches that this is truly propitiatory and has this effect, that if we, contrite and penitent, with sincere heart and upright faith, with fear and reverence, draw nigh to God, we obtain mercy and find grace in seasonable aid (Heb. 4:16).

Interestingly, chapter 8 of this work says that the Mass may not be celebrated in the vernacular tongue, though its mysteries should be explained to the common people. This teaching was plainly altered by Vatican II (1962–1965).

Modern Catholic thought on these matters has changed only very slightly from what we read above. *The Catechism of the Catholic Church* states, "The holy Eucharist completes Christian initiation. Those who have been raised to the dignity of the royal priesthood by baptism and configured more deeply to Christ by Confirmation participate with the whole community in the Lord's own sacrifice by means of the Eucharist."[4]

This same modern catechism adds,

> The Eucharist is "the source and summit of the Christian life.... The other sacraments, and indeed all ecclesiastical

> ministries and works of the apostolate, are bound up with the Eucharist and are oriented toward it. For in the blessed Eucharist is contained the whole spiritual good of the Church, namely Christ himself, our Pasch [Paschal Lamb]."

A few sentences later, the Mass is said to be "the sum and substance of our faith."[5]

It is imperative that evangelical readers understand that without the Mass a Catholic has no religion, no faith to practice, and no communion or mystical fellowship with Christ. It is for the discerning Catholic "The Blessed Sacrament." It is a sacrament because the worshiper, according to the Catholic teaching, is nourished by the body and blood of Christ—Christ is actually received by the Catholic worshiper. It is a sacrifice because a gift is offered to God. Christ is offered by the priest, on behalf of the congregation, to God the Father.

In the words of one devout Catholic friend, who eventually came to a different understanding of the mystery of the Mass, "I would often kneel before the consecrated host, which was carefully placed in a monstrance and set upon the altar for display in the church sanctuary.... during those times of silent prayer before the 'Blessed Sacrament' I felt, literally, as though I was kneeling before Jesus Himself." This deep expression of the mystery and wonder of worship is not understood by those who have never been faithful Roman Catholics.

But does Catholic theology see the Mass as a separate sacrifice from that of the cross, as some Protestants have written? No. What is actually taught is that the sacrifice of Calvary is one and the same as the sacrifice of the Mass. It is believed that the same victim and the same offering as that of Calvary is sacramentally, mysteriously, present on the altar of the Mass. As one pope has defined it: "The august sacrfice of the altar, then, is no mere commemoration of the passion and death of Jesus Christ, but a true and proper act of sacrifice, whereby the High Priest by an unbloody immolation [i.e., by the act of sacrificial death] he offers Himself a most acceptable victim to the Eternal Father, as He did upon the cross."[6]

Thus, Roman Catholic dogma denies that the Mass is simply a dramatic reenactment or commemoration of Christ's death. It is a real sacrifice that continues the eternal sacrifice of Christ, which is above time. Contemporary Catholic apologist Karl Keating says, "Although Christ died only once, through the Mass his saving act is made actually present, day by day, until the end of the world."[7]

The faithful Catholic must take the Mass at least once a year. He must be in a state of grace when he takes the Mass; that is, without unconfessed mortal sin. Many modern American Catholics must think that they rarely commit a mortal sin because the practice of confession has declined in recent years. In this, American Catholics are fundamentally wrong according to the dogma of their own church.

For a sin to be mortal, three requirements must be met. Writes Catholic apologist Karl Keating, "First, it must be a serious matter. Second, there must be sufficient reflection on its seriousness. And, third, there must be full consent in the committing of it."[8] What exactly is a "serious matter"? Any sin contrary to the Ten Commandments or the moral teaching of the church can qualify: murder, adultery, envy, abortion, artificial birth control, thievery, sodomy, fornication, stealing, and lying all fit the category.

Finally, one of the most important and distinctive elements of the Roman Catholic doctrine of the Mass is what is called transubstantiation. In this teaching it is believed that the bread and wine in the Mass are converted (changed) into the body and blood of Christ Himself. The whole substance of the bread and wine is converted into the whole substance of Christ's body, but without the appearance changing. The bread still looks like bread and tastes like bread, but it is really, fundamentally, actually, the flesh of Jesus. Simply put, in the Mass Christ's whole body and blood exist wholly and entirely in every part of the consecrated bread and wine. This teaching has ancient roots, but it goes beyond the Scriptures' plain teaching.

The Mass is more than an evangelical eucharist ("thanksgiving") or a simple Lord's Supper celebration, wherein we nurture our faith by the elements that point us to Christ and strengthen faith in Him. This can't be said too clearly—in the Catholic mystery the Mass is the *supreme* moment in the worship of the church. This is the time when the priest offers Christ as a sacrifice for the living and the dead. In this sense Christ is on the altar, offered up before God the Father and the people in a sacrifice contiguous with Calvary. That is why Catholics bow, venerate, and adore the host (Latin, "victim") in the Mass—this is Jesus Christ before the eyes of faith. They believe they are showing reverence to Christ Himself. If Christ does indeed become real in body and blood before the worshipers gathered, then this reverence is correct.

When Catholics take the host they sincerely believe that they eat the body of Jesus Christ, which is *indispensable* for their salvation. That is also why the priest raises the host before the flock and declares, "This is the Lamb of God who takes away the sin of the world." The *Catechism of the Catholic Church* says the consecrated bread and wine are heavenly foods that actually help the devout to attain salvation. It is stated this way:

> What material food produces in our bodily life, Holy Communion wonderfully achieves in our spiritual life. Communion with the flesh of the risen Christ . . . preserves, increases, and renews the life of grace received at Baptism. . . . Every time this mystery is celebrated, "the work of our redemption is carried on" and we "break the one bread that provides the medicine of immortality, the antidote for death, and the food that makes us live for ever in Jesus Christ."[9]

One former Catholic, nurtured in the doctrine and practice of the Mass, put it this way:

> From early in my childhood I was taught to genuflect toward the tabernacle (the receptacle in which the consecrated hosts were stored until the next Mass) out of respect for God. I served on the altar as an altar boy from third grade through my junior year in high school. During Mass, when the priest would elevate the host and chalice, and say, "Behold the Lamb of God, who takes away the sin of the world," I would bow my head and pray to Jesus, believing He was now right in front of me! Such feelings do not pass away easily.

The Origins of the Mass

Paul Johnson, a noted British writer, historian, and Roman Catholic churchman, has written a most useful book titled *The History of Christianity*. In this work, Johnson looks at how Christianity changed to meet the public opinion of the first four centuries. He writes that the church "in the second [century] had acquired the elements of ecclesiastical organization; in the third it created an intellectual and philosophical structure; and in the fourth, especially in the later half of the century, it built up a dramatic and impressive public persona: it began to think and act like a state church."[10]

As the dress of the nobleman became the dress of bishops, reactions came from both those who favored change and those who opposed it. The church began to take on forms and practices that were beyond its simple and humble origins in first-century Jewish culture. In addition, new practices were adopted and doctrines developed that explained, defended, and defined these practices. Some of these changes might well have been harmless and even useful to an extent. But the problem is the church has always had the tendency to adopt the pattern of the world, of other religions, or of state governments and political forces.

With the Mass a doctrine evolved that explained the mysteries now accepted as biblical by modern Catholics. Johnson, himself a Catholic, is again helpful:

> The basic framework of the mass had already existed in the mid-second century, when it was described by Justin Martyr. It consisted of readings from the memoirs of the apostles and the Old Testament; a sermon; a prayer followed by the kiss of peace and the distribution of the blessed bread and water. This Sunday eucharist had become an absolute obligation by Justin's time and the words of the central prayer became formalized in the next generation or two. . . . The effect . . . was to change an essentially simple ceremony into a much lengthier and more formal one, involving an element of grandeur. . . . Some of the ceremonial aspects were taken over from pagan rites, others from court practice, which became far more elaborate after the transfer to Constantinople. . . . The object was to replace the magnificence of pagan ritual in the public mind, also partly to win the struggle against Arianism. . . . At the end of the fourth century John Chrysostom spoke of the Lord's table as "a place of terror and shuddering," not to be seen by profane eyes, and it became customary to screen it with curtains . . . whose effect was to hide all the operations on the altar from the congregation as a whole, and to deepen the chasm between clergy and laity.[11]

As early as the second and third century the Mass began to be referred to by some church theologians as a *sacrifice.* Some spoke of it as the commemoration of Christ's passion, while others began to write of it as an actual offering in reparation for sins. By the Middle Ages the church, having borrowed both philosophically and religiously from numerous sources, could speak of the Mass at the Council of Trent as a bloodless sacrifice. In 1215, after three centuries of often intense debate, the church at the Lateran Council accepted the idea that during the Mass the bread and wine become the body and blood of Christ (transubstantiation).

In ancient ritual blood sacrifices (in pagan religions) the worshiper must consume the blood of the victim as a sacrifice. This idea was incorporated in such a manner that now the communing believer takes the bread (the body of Christ) into his own flesh in this the supreme moment of Christian worship. This becomes the central mystery of the Catholic's faith and practice—the eating of the body of Christ.

The Mass was enshrined in an elaborate ritual, in time, much like a "rare gem in a costly setting," as one historian put it. When the priest spoke the appointed words over the bread and wine a miracle took place. The miracle was transubstantiation. The broken body and outpoured blood are offered up to God as a sacrifice for the living and the dead. The liturgy reaches its apex when the "host" (the consecrated wafer, now Christ's body) is lifted high in the air, and the Mass bell rung. Here the worshiper prostrates himself in humility before the physically present Savior, Christ Jesus Himself. In past ages, where superstition abounded, miracles were frequently associated with these moments in the Mass. In my visits to Latin America I have seen this same kind of phenomenon claimed in our age.

As noted earlier, until Vatican II the Mass was not said in the language of the people. The priest did not face the congregation, and usually the cup was not given to the communicants, since the bread was the body of Christ itself. Much of this has changed since 1965. What has *not* changed is the fundamental nature of the Mass as a sacrifice in which Christ is believed to be present in the bread and wine. True and devout Catholics still believe that Christ is physically present in the bread and wine. Thus they cannot conceive of salvation apart from receiving the mystery of their faith in the body and blood of Christ. This teaching, therefore, has powerful influence over the whole perception of what constitutes acceptable Christian worship.

The Teaching of the New Testament

An appeal to the New Testament is often not enough for the faithful Roman Catholic. Why is this so? Because the magisterium of the church is considered to be the highest authority in matters of faith and practice. We cannot escape the delineating character of "Scripture alone" no matter how much we seek to understand and explain our real differences. We really do have two entirely *different* authorities for faith and practice. And nothing underscores this problem more than the mystery of the Mass.

But what do I mean by "the magisterium"? This is the church's teaching authority. It is believed that this authority was instituted by Christ Himself and has been guided by the Holy Spirit down through the ages. Its task is to safeguard the truth and interpret it properly for the faithful. This authority is exercised in two ways: *extraordinary*—popes and councils infallibly define truth or morals that are necessary for one's salvation and that have been constantly taught and held by the church over the ages; *ordinary*—the church infallibly defines the truths of the faith. These are truths that are 1) taught universally and without dissent, 2) taught or the magisterium would fail in its duty, 3) connected with a grave matter of faith or morals, and 4) taught authoritatively. Not everything taught by the magisterium is done so infallibly; however, it is believed that the exercise of the magisterium is faithful to Christ and what He taught (cf. entry in Our Sunday Visitor's *Catholic Dictionary*).

When the evangelical Reformers raised their protest against the practices of the sixteenth-century church, they made much of the need for a complete doctrinal and practical reform in public worship. John Calvin, the great Swiss Reformer, believed that the church's worship had become "gross idolatry" by the time of the Middle Ages and that this practice needed as much attention in the cause of true reformation as the doctrine of justification by faith. Calvin wished to replace what he called the "godly show" with a simple, radically biblical, public service of worship that was developed according to the revealed patterns of the New Testament Scriptures.

Robert Godfrey, a historian of the Protestant Reformation, sums up the concern of Reformers such as John Calvin:

> Calvin laments that the simplicity of sacramental doctrine and practice that prevailed in the early church had been lost. This is most clearly seen in the Lord's Supper. Eucharistic sacrifice, transubstantiation, and the worship of the consecrated bread and wine are unbiblical and destroy the real meaning of the sacrament. "While the sacrament ought to be a means of raising pious minds to heaven, the sacred symbols of the Supper were abused to an entirely different purpose, and men, contented with gazing upon them and worshipping them, never once thought of Christ." The work of Christ is destroyed, as can be seen in the ideal of eucharistic sacrifice, where "Christ was sacrificed a thousand times a day, as if he had not done enough in once dying for us."[12]

For Calvin, who developed a biblical theology of the Lord's Supper that carefully followed the text of the New Testament, the elements did not become the actual body and blood of Christ physically, nor was Christ sacrificed on the altar for the people. Rather, true believers, when they came to communion, ate and drank in faith, believing that Christ was spiritually present with them in the fellowship of His appointed meal. He could not be seen, for His body was physically in heaven, but His Spirit was there in the fellowship of His people communing with them through the visible signs. This seems, quite simply, to be the correct rendering of the meaning of 1 Corinthians 10:16 and 11:17-26, the two critical apostolic texts on the Lord's Supper that exist outside the institution of the meal by our Lord (see also Matthew 26:26-29; Mark 14:22–25; Luke 22:14-23).

Consider for a moment our Lord's institution of the Supper as recorded in Matthew 26:26-29. First, Jesus takes the bread and wine, saying that these were His body and blood. Did any of those present have any idea of something like transubstantiation? Did they not hear His words exactly as we read them in the text itself? Jesus was standing in their very presence. He had not yet died! After they had drunk the wine they heard Him say, "I will not drink of this fruit of the vine from now on until that day when I drink it anew with you in my Father's kingdom" (verse 29). He did not say, "I will not drink My blood." If only the appearance of the wine remained but the reality was now blood, we would surely expect Him to make this clear to His own disciples. That the disciples understood this drink of the fruit of the vine to be symbolic of Christ's death through the shedding of His blood seems quite apparent in the text.

In teaching that the "substance" changes in the elements of the Mass, while the outward "accidents" do not, Catholicism actually falls into serious contradiction. Is not the inward nature of the object that which truly produces the outward appearance? Further, where in Scripture is there a miracle where the outward appearance remains unchanged but those who observe the miracle are expected to believe that a real miracle has actually taken place? To suggest that God deals with mankind in this manner raises serious problems. It is not a question of "having enough faith," but rather of "what is the proper object of faith"?

In addition, when we read the gospel passages about the actual institution of the Lord's Supper, we discover that the language is plainly figurative. The teaching of Jesus on that last evening with His disciples is given in fullest measure in John 13–17. Here, throughout this entire evening, we discover that figures of speech abound. Further, the apostles were Jews, and Jews had strict dietary laws—laws that clearly prohibited their eating foods that still contained blood (see Acts 15:28-29). Years after the Lord had instituted this special meal, Peter says, "I have never eaten anything impure or unclean" (Acts 10:14). If he had been eating and drinking the body and blood of Christ for several years, it is highly doubtful that he would have said this.

Jesus had promised to be with His own throughout the ages (see John 14:16-18). He was going to send the Holy Spirit, who would make Him known to them. Christ's presence is not in buildings or rituals. He is with His people when they do what He commands. He is blessing them and revealing His presence to them when they keep His commandments. The two signs (visible commandments) that He has given to His gathered people are baptism and the Lord's Supper. When we eat and drink in remembrance of Him, He is there, but not *physically* in the bread and wine. He is there by the Holy Spirit, strengthening the faith of His people as they commune with Him in obedience to His commandments.

If Holy Communion is not a real sacrifice or the eating of the real body of Christ, what is it? In 1 Corinthians 10:21 Paul calls the cup "the cup of the Lord." He speaks of our drinking it as "a sharing in" (Gk. *koinonia*, "fellowship"; verse 16) with the Lord. Later, in 1 Corinthians 11:17-34, the apostle teaches that in this meal God's people gather to remember the greatest display of love ever given them. As a result of this powerful remembrance of Christ they are to love one another, something that they were not doing very well in Corinth. As a spiritual family they were to gather at this table to celebrate Christ's grace and mercy for them and to be united in love for Him and each other. Here they were to remember Him "until He comes." This is the simple meaning of the meal that Christ gave to His church. No amount of tradition should be allowed to tamper with these truths plainly set forth in the text of Scripture.

Summing Up

The Last Supper of our Lord was, when read in its appropriate New Testament context, clearly a Passover meal. Christ's own blood was about to be poured out, in a matter of hours, for the forgiveness of sins. As Peter himself wrote, "He Himself [i.e., Christ] bore our sins in his body on the tree" (1 Peter 2:24). Further, upon a simple reading of the text of Scripture, it is evident that the bread and the wine are plainly *symbols* of Christ's body and blood:

> For I received from the Lord what I also passed on to you: The Lord Jesus, on the night he was betrayed, took bread, and when he had given thanks, he broke it and said, "This is my body, which is for you; do this in remembrance of me." In the same way, after supper he took the cup, saying, "This cup is the new covenant in my blood; do this, whenever you drink it, in remembrance of me." For whenever you eat this bread and drink this cup, you proclaim the Lord's death until he comes (1 Corinthians 11:23-26).

By these symbols, namely the bread and the wine, we *remember* Christ and His sacrifice for us (see also Luke 22:19). Furthermore, Christ's body is not presently on the church altar in the Mass, for His glorified and raised body is now present in heaven. The writer of Hebrews puts it this way:

> When this priest had offered for all time one sacrifice for sins, he sat down at the right hand of God [here the writer clearly has in mind the death of Jesus Christ]. Since that time he waits for his enemies to be made his footstool, because by one sacrifice he has made perfect forever those who are being made holy (Hebrews 10:12-14).

The body of Christ was sacrificed once, nearly 2,000 years ago, in the historical event of the cross outside the ancient city of Jerusalem (see Mark 15:21-41). When our Lord said, in His death, "It is finished" (John 19:30), was it *really* finished? Was His unique death sufficient for the sins of *all* who believe throughout *all* the ages or was it not? Hebrews is again very clear on this point:

> For Christ did not enter a man-made sanctuary that was only a copy of the true one; he entered heaven itself, now to appear for us in God's presence. Nor did he enter heaven to offer himself again and again, the way the high priest enters the Most Holy Place every year with blood that is not his own. Then Christ would have had to suffer many times since the creation of the world. But now he has appeared once for all at the end of the ages to do away with sin by the sacrifice of himself. Just as man is destined to die once, and after that to face judgment, so Christ was sacrificed once to take away the sins of many people; and he will appear a second time, not to bear sin, but to bring salvation to those waiting for him (Hebrews 9:24-28).

Please observe, dear reader, that a straightforward reading of these words allows for no *repeated* offerings of Christ. His offering and sacrifice is complete, once for all time. He has paid fully the penalty of sin (death) and thus done "away with sin by the sacrifice of himself." Seven times, from Hebrews 7:27 through 10:14, the writer speaks of the uniqueness of Christ's death by using clear language such as "once for all time" or "by one sacrifice." No matter how modern Catholicism presents this mystery to your heart, this understanding does serious violence to the clear meaning of sacred Scripture. The Lord took upon Himself the totality of the sins of all who believe in His Son. He "bore the sins of the many, and made intercession for the transgressors" (Isaiah 53:12).

If you are a practicing Catholic and consider yourself to also be a person of evangelical faith in Christ, you must carefully consider your profession of faith in the light of the plain Catholic dogma of the Mass. Your church teaches that you must be in full agreement with the mystery of this doctrine.

You are not to receive the elements if you cannot do so in true faith. You are required to say an "Amen" when the priest says to the congregation, "The body of Christ." This "Amen" is a solemn Hebrew word which means, "It is so, this is the body of Christ!" The church seriously exhorts you to refrain from taking the communion if you do not agree with her. At the same time you cannot escape the force of Holy Scripture upon your own conscience. You must decide this utterly serious matter before God and His Word. To God alone you will answer at the end of this present age.

I understand how the heart and soul of devout Catholics must struggle with what has been said about the mystery of the Mass and the actual teaching of Scripture. This is the heart and soul of your Catholic experience of Christ and the church. A dear friend expresses well what you may well feel at this point: "Sometimes it is hard to be completely objective in this area of doctrine. The emotional ties run so very deep. . . . my mind reads these texts and understands them but my emotions still struggle profoundly."

Soak your mind and heart in the sacred Scriptures. Ask the Holy Spirit to reveal the truth to your heart. Be willing to test everything by the Word of God. Here alone will you find peace and safety, both now and in the day of judgment.

CHAPTER SIX

Seven Sacraments

As we saw in an earlier chapter, Roman Catholicism has seven sacraments. Evangelicals have only two—baptism and communion. Both the number of the sacraments and the definition, or nature, of each is a subject that further displays some of the deep differences that remain between evangelical Christians and Roman Catholics. In this chapter we will look at the Roman Catholic definition of a sacrament, drawing our definitions from standard Catholic sources. Finally, we will try to better understand why the church teaches that these seven sacraments are at the very core of the Catholic mystery. We will also seek to understand what each sacrament means to the faith of the devout Catholic.

A Crucial Understanding

As with the Mass, the six other sacraments in Catholic practice hinge ultimately upon the doctrine of the authority of the church. The church appeals to Scripture in the definition of each of the seven sacraments, but the church's historically evolving understanding of each came to fruition in a past council or a papal decision that *ultimately* defined what the Catholic understanding of a particular sacrament is. In other words, it is believed that the seed for the practice *is* in Scripture, but the flower comes to bloom, as it were, through the work of the teaching authority of the magisterium. In Catholic practice doctrinal understanding develops and "the acorn becomes a tree" in the development of specific dogma. This observation is plainly stated in the new *Catechism of the Catholic Church*: "As she has done for the canon of sacred Scripture and for the doctrine of the faith, the Church, by the power of the Spirit who guides her 'into all truth,' has gradually recognized this treasure... and has determined its 'dispensation.'"[1]

When evangelicals are drawn to Catholicism, or when Catholics consider their own faith and practice in the light of evangelical beliefs, certain factors become powerfully attractive. For this reason we cannot respond to the matter of the sacraments simply by appealing to history and the creeds. We need to understand the actual doctrine, as Catholicism teaches it, asking at each point, "What is the biblical warrant for this teaching?"

What Exactly Is a Sacrament?

Sacraments are defining characteristics for the mystery that is Roman Catholicism; that is, without them there really would be no Roman Catholicism. In sacramental religion, grace comes to the soul not directly but in a *mediated* manner. In contrast, the evangelical generally thinks in terms of God coming to him directly by the ministry of the Holy Spirit *through* the Word of God. (Many evangelicals, though not all, believe God does give grace *through* the means of the Lord's Supper but only to the one who has saving faith.) But the faithful Catholic thinks of God coming to him through the sacramental ministry of the church. He comes particularly through the seven sacraments. This is why sacramental life is at the heart of the Catholic mystery.

In Catholic thought, salvation is understood in terms of the descent of a higher reality. Catholic teaching clearly has a place for the merit of Christ atoning for human sin, but when this teaching is mixed with the mystical notions of the Catholic faith in the context of sacramental life, the implication is that something higher or deeper than Christ's atonement saves. (The historical death of Christ is what saves, as we saw in the last chapter, bringing the sinner into personal salvation through the agency of the Spirit.) In the sacraments God actually comes down and lifts up the sinner, who receives His grace. This makes him a partaker of the divine nature *through* the mystery of the church.

But what exactly is a sacrament? According to the Council of Trent, a sacrament is an "effective sign of grace instituted by Christ." The new *Catechism of the Catholic Church* maintains this same centuries-old teaching: "The whole liturgical life of the Church revolves around the Eucharistic sacrifice and the sacraments"; and, further:

> "Jesus' words and actions during his hidden life and public ministry were already salvific.... They announced and prepared what he was going to give the Church when all was accomplished. The mysteries of Christ's life are the foundations of what he would henceforth dispense in the sacraments."[2]

It is also imperative that we understand the power and saving role these sacraments have for the life of the believing Catholic. Most evangelicals who discuss this with Catholics have little idea of the teaching of the Roman Church. The *Catechism of the Catholic Church* concludes, "Celebrated worthily in faith, the sacraments confer the grace that they signify. They are efficacious because in them Christ himself is at work: it is he who baptizes, he who acts in his sacraments in order to communicate the grace that each sacrament signifies."[3]

All this is understood by the faithful Catholic to mean that a sacrament is more than a sign that declares, or points to, the reality. It *is* the reality; it *actually effects* in the heart of baptized believers something of God's grace. This is the idea behind the argument which surrounds the Latin phrase *ex opere operato*—that is, by virtue of the performance of the act grace is actually given.

The essentials of a Catholic sacrament, by definition, are three. First, there is the *matter*. This refers to the physical substance itself (in the case of penance or marriage the action perceived by the human senses is the matter). Second, there is the *form*. This refers to the words employed, which are determined by the church and must not be altered. Finally, there is a minister with the *right intention*. When these essentials are present you have, according to Catholic teaching, a valid sacrament.

More recent Catholic teaching, in distinction from the Council of Trent, seems quite intent on saying that faith must reside in the one who receives the sacrament or the sacrament is not effective. The argument is that sacraments presuppose faith in some sense, but in words as well as in objects they are still said to nourish, strengthen, and express faith mystically. There is a definite improvement in terms of doctrinal development, but the evangelical is still troubled by the idea of a sacrament *effecting what it represents*. How can grace actually be imparted *via* a sacrament?

Take baptism as a significant example. The Catholic doctrine is this: Baptism not only represents the cleansing of the soul from sin, but it actually effects the cleansing in the action of the sacrament. Says the *Catechism of the Catholic Church*, "Baptism not only purifies from all sins, but also makes the neophyte 'a new creature,' an adopted son of God, who has become a 'partaker of the divine nature,' member of Christ and co-heir with him, and a temple of the Holy Spirit."[4] Very simply put, baptism conveys actual grace and saves the person who receives it. He is made a child of God in the action of the baptism. The *Catechism* adds, "Baptism makes us members of the Body of Christ. . . . From the baptismal font is born the one people of God."[5]

Because of such teaching, my earlier reference to the phrase *ex opere operato* is not out of line. Indeed, the same modern *Catechism of the Catholic Church* summarizes the church's sacramental teaching this way:

> Celebrated worthily in faith, the sacraments confer the grace that they signify. They are efficacious because in them Christ himself is at work: it is he who baptizes, he who acts in the sacraments in order to communicate the grace that each sacrament signifies. The Father always hears the prayer of the Son's Church which, in the [divine calling] of each sacrament, expresses her faith in the power of the Spirit. As fire transforms into itself everything it touches, so the Holy Spirit transforms into the divine life whatever is subjected to his power. This is the meaning of the Church's affirmation that the sacraments act *ex opere operato* (literally "by the very fact of the action's being performed"), i.e., by virtue of the saving work of Christ, accomplished once for all. It follows that the sacrament is not wrought by the righteousness of either the celebrant or the recipient, but by the power of God. From the moment a sacrament is celebrated in accordance with the intention of the Church, the power of Christ and his Spirit acts in and through it, independently of the personal holiness of the minister. Nevertheless, the fruits of the sacraments also depend on the disposition of the one who receives them.[6]

So sacraments "confer grace." They really are "efficacious." By analogy, as fire transforms everything it touches, so the Spirit uses sacraments to transform all that the sacraments touch, and, in the aforementioned sense, this clearly is *ex opere operato*; that is, the thing is actually accomplished by the sacrament.

What Are the Seven Sacraments?

Roman Catholic theology teaches that the number of sacraments is seven. What are these seven sacraments, and how does Catholic theology define them? Each definition that follows is paraphrased from the *Catholic Encyclopedia* (Our Sunday Visitor). My intention is to properly represent an official understanding of the Catholic position.

1. *Baptism.* The sacrament in which the one baptized is cleansed of original sin and (in the case of one who has reached the age of reason) of particular sin; he is incorporated into Christ and made a member of His Body the church; he is infused with sanctifying grace and receives the theological virtues of faith, hope, and love and the gifts of the Holy Spirit; and this enables him to receive the other sacraments effectively. The minister of baptism is ordinarily a bishop, priest, or deacon, but in an emergency anyone can baptize validly. There is also the "baptism of blood" (which is martyrdom for the faith) and the "baptism of desire" (which is baptism credited to a person who had perfect contrition and implicit intention but for whatever reason could not have been baptized).

2. *Confirmation.* This sacrament is said to have been instituted by Christ when He promised to send His Holy Spirit and it was fulfilled in Pentecost. When it is asked, "What must I do to be saved?" the answer given in Acts 2:37-38 suggests a twofold aspect: first, baptism for the forgiveness of sins; second, confirmation for the Spirit to be given. It is said, further, that Acts 8 and 19 provide scriptural witness to confirmation after baptism through a laying on of hands and reception of the Holy Spirit. Contemporary Catholic theology sees confirmation as the completion of baptism, a sealing with the Spirit, which enables witness to the Christian faith in a mature way. For this reason confirmation and first communion are extremely important points in the life of young Catholic children and their families.

3. *Holy Eucharist.* From the Greek *eucharistia*, meaning "thanksgiving," this is the sacrament of the body and blood of Christ, in which He is presented under the forms of bread and wine, offering Himself in the sacrifice of the Mass and giving Himself as spiritual food to the faithful. The *Catholic Encyclopedia*,

demonstrating what we saw in chapter 5, adds, "Because of the importance and holiness invested in it by Christ Himself, the Eucharist is the chief act of worship in the Catholic Church, and the Consecrated Species of the Eucharist are to be adored by the faithful with the same worship due to God, because of Christ's substantial presence."[7]

4. *Penance.* Popularly called "confession," this is also referred to as the sacrament of reconciliation (more accurately the "rite of reconciliation and the sacrament of penance"). The church, according to this doctrine, has been given the power, by Christ, to forgive sin. This sacrament is based on a three-dimensional concept of sin. Sin affects ourselves, our relationship with God, and our relationship with the church of Christ.

The Council of Trent defended penance against the opposition of the Protestant Reformers, who saw the priest as unnecessary for granting forgiveness. Trent, in response, required Catholics to confess all mortal sin by species (type of sin) and number (approximate) to a priest, who would then absolve them in the name of Christ and the Catholic Church. Vatican II reformed this practice slightly by stressing the healing aspects of penance. The new rite is celebrated either individually or communally (i.e., for several at once). This latter form is intended to display the community aspects of sin and reconciliation. Present Catholic canon law obliges all Catholics to confess mortal sins by species and number at least once a year and encourages the confessing of venial sins as well.

5. *Anointing of the Sick.* This sacrament was once referred to as "extreme unction" (from the Latin "to smear" or "to anoint"). Formerly the sacrament was primarily for the dying, since it was administered only in extreme situations. It was even described as "the last rites." Several other sacraments actually include anointings—baptism, confirmation, and ordination. This sacrament is said to give strengthening grace and is thus no longer exclusively used for dying people. The idea behind this anointing is to offer God's healing grace to the infirm and the

aged, to remit sin, and to make known the prayerful solicitude of the entire body of Christ for those beset by illness or ailment.

6. *Holy Orders.* This is the sacrament in which a bishop imposes his hands upon a man and uses a prescribed prayer to confer spiritual power and grace to conduct ordained ministry in the Catholic Church. It is believed to put an "indelible mark" upon the soul of the recipient and thus can be received only once. Within this one sacrament are three orders: 1) diaconate, 2) priesthood, and 3) episcopate. Each is administered separately and with successively higher sacramental powers.

Deacons are ordained to a ministry of service and, in communion with priests and bishops, serve in the liturgy (service of worship). Priests are ordained with the power to celebrate the Mass, give absolution to penitents, administer the sacraments, preach and teach the Word of God, and fulfill pastoral duties given by their superiors. (In America and Europe a debate rages over whether or not women should receive holy orders and serve in the priesthood, a position that the Vatican has consistently rejected.) Bishops receive the sacrament as a fullness of their priesthood and are viewed as successors to the apostles; thus they alone have the sacramental power to ordain others. A bishop cares for the church under his particular charge as well as for the universal church.

7. *Marriage.* This sacrament was officially recognized as such at the Fourth Lateran Council in 1215. Theologically it is considered a sacrament because it reflects Christ's union with His bride, the church. Unlike other sacraments, marriage predated Christ, but it is believed that He lifted it to sacramental status by His teaching and practice. Marriage is recognized as an institution of nature, good for all; but for Catholics who receive it properly in the fellowship of the church it is a sacrament because it is viewed as a means of encountering Christ in a special way and of bringing about the salvation of spouses.

For marriage to be a sacrament, Catholic couples must remove any impediments that might exist. It is here that the whole matter of the annulment of a previous marriage comes up, as well as related issues that often involve priests in matters that are difficult to pastorally administer. (This has caused increasing numbers of Catholics in America to pull away from the visible church after going through a divorce.) Both Vatican II and more recent papal documents have addressed the ever-changing need for better understanding of this doctrine.

An Examination in Light of Biblical Teaching

The Roman Catholic understanding of salvation, as we have seen, is plainly linked to the mystery of sacramentalism, which has been called "sacerdotalism" (of, or relating to, priests and/or the priesthood). To the average person who has not carefully studied the New Testament or considered the effect of this system upon whole nations of untaught baptized church members, this system carries a certain appeal. It has the appearance of awe, of mystery, of wonder—all elements of true Christian worship. But for those who resolve to follow Scripture alone and believe the doctrine of the sufficiency of Christ alone and the gospel alone, there are serious problems with the entire system. These problems cannot be resolved easily by goodwill and ecumenical discussion.

As previously noted, evangelicals have historically held that there are but two sacraments clearly instituted by our Lord in the New Testament. In the case of baptism we have an explicit commandment of Christ to practice this act until He comes again. Jesus commanded His church to "go and make disciples of all the nations, baptizing them in the name of the Father and the Son and the Holy Spirit" (Matthew 28:19). To obey Christ's command, the church has always baptized those who follow Christ as Lord. There has been disagreement among evangelicals regarding both the meaning and mode of baptism, but all agree that Christ Himself commanded baptism.

In the case of communion we have an account of the institution of the Supper by our Lord Himself. When the apostle Paul tells the church in Corinth to celebrate the Supper he quotes Jesus as saying, "This is My body, which is for you; do this in remembrance of me" (1 Corinthians 11:24). The Savior exhorts His followers to do this in order to remember Him. Nothing could be plainer and more straightforward.

Where, then, are we to find textual support for the five remaining sacraments? Did Christ command any of these in the *same* manner and with the *same* authority as the two sacraments just mentioned? I think not. I have read the scriptural texts cited in Catholic sources for the other sacraments, and I am left with a number of unanswered questions.

For example, where did Christ Himself institute these in a manner that parallels baptism and the Lord's Supper? If He did not institute them, *how* were they instituted as sacraments? (The Catholic Church has sometimes argued that they were instituted by the apostles, but this legitimation is not *clearly* found in Scripture either.) History cannot show that these sacraments were directly instituted by Christ, yet the Council of Trent, in responding to Protestant doctrine, said that it could. Honesty compels me to ask my Catholic friends to recognize that the ultimate claim for these five additional sacraments is actually the authority of the church. This authority, we will see, is focused on a triad of the Bible, tradition, and the magisterium.

Further, the Catholic system of authority, with its attendant sacerdotalism, generally makes the Scriptures secondary, or subordinate, to these sacramental means of grace. Popular modern Catholic apologists often argue otherwise, but reality begs for a more honest answer. I would ask my American Catholic friends to travel with me to Brazil. Here they would observe the reality of Catholic practice among the masses as people flock to the shrines and holy places and wait for the grace of God to come down to them through the sacerdotal system of their birth church.

But evangelicals have consistently maintained since the Reformation that the sacraments (even the two that Scripture plainly enumerates) *add nothing* to salvation at all. Salvation is grasped by faith alone in the promises of God, a faith that comes to us supernaturally by the Holy Spirit using the Word of God. The written Word is a vast treasure in which the promises of God are contained and discovered by be-lieving hearts. It has God for its Author and truth for its entire substance.

Despite the many dramatic changes made by Vatican II (1962–1965), the traditional Catholic doctrine of the sacraments remains fundamentally unchanged. (That is why I have used post-Vatican II sources in all my notations above.) These seven sacraments are received as a means of direct access to God. Simply put, these seven sacraments truly define the Catholic mystery itself.

The apostle Peter expresses the evangelical view of the *means* of salvation plainly: "You have been born again, not of perishable seed, but of imperishable, through the living and enduring word of God" (1 Peter 1:23). The verses that follow this text make it plain that the word he has in view is the word preached by the apostles and ultimately inscripturated in the New Testament writings.

In addition, the New Testament nowhere gives warrant to the idea that sacraments are *necessary* for salvation. I offer three reasons for this assertion:

1. *God nowhere binds His grace to the use of certain external forms.* Consider the following texts in this light: Luke 18:14; John 4:21,23. Further, the New Testament has a strong anti-ritualistic element that can be clearly seen over and over again (see Matthew 15; Romans 14:17; 1 Corinthians 1:17; 8:8; Colossians 2:16-23; Hebrews 9:10; 13:9-16; 1 Peter 3:21).

2. *Scripture makes faith alone the instrumental cause of salvation* (John 5:24; see also 3:16,36; Acts 16:31). Verses that appear to say otherwise are best read in the light of the clearer texts and the simple principle that is defined and defended in

Romans and Galatians. The *objective* efficacy attributed to the sacraments, even if it is called "applicatory" in certain places, implies an addition to the finished work of the Lord Jesus Christ in His death, burial, and resurrection. The question is this: Did Jesus fully accomplish the objective side of our salvation in His death, burial, and resurrection? If the answer is yes, then no further sacrifice is needed, and any notion of the works of human merit, albeit made meritorious through infused grace, is completely foreign to the teachings of the New Testament.

3. *The sacraments do not originate faith*. They are not administered in order that faith will be *created* by them: Acts 2:41; 16:14-15,30,33; 1 Corinthians 11:23-32.

Summing Up

Roman Catholic theology and faith display an entirely different view of Christian salvation and faith than that of the New Testament. The church, in Catholic theology, is seen as an extension of Christ's incarnation and sacrifice. In this system, human agents are given power that belongs to God alone (that is, priests absolving sin, giving grace through sacraments, and so on).

In evangelical faith, which follows the straightforward words of Scripture, true faith answers to the Word of God alone and takes the promises of Scripture as its own. This is based upon the "bare" word of God alone, not church traditions. Christ's expiatory (atoning) sacrifice is a once-for-all event. He is the perfect substitute. For the Christian who would follow the New Testament, the real need is to take Him in faith and trust Him alone to save. The mystery of sacramental life cannot save. That is Christ's role, and His alone; and He saves through the agency of His Word and Spirit.

CHAPTER SEVEN

Who Really Speaks for God?

Serious evangelical dialogue with Roman Catholicism finds it virtually impossible to avoid the issues raised by the institution of the papacy. These issues were central in the sixteenth-century division, and they remain problematic for modern discussion. It is hard for Catholics in the West to understand the serious concern evangelicals have regarding the papacy, since they often think of John Paul II as a benevolent and gracious gentleman who warmly radiates love for Christ and for all non-Catholics.

In a special commentary on the Feast Day (1971) honoring St. Peter and St. Paul, the Vatican radio declared, "The Church does not exist without the pope. The pope does not exist without the Church. He who believes in the Church believes in the pope. He who believes in the pope believes in the Church. Pope and Church are inseparable realities." This understanding, which sounds so completely foreign to the evangelical mind, is perfectly natural to Catholic teaching, with its fully developed doctrine of ecclesiastical authority.

That the Roman Catholic Church is a hierarchical organization, with the bishops at the top of the structure, is the very essence of Catholicism. In fact, the central idea of church authority, as Rome understands it, lies in the office of the bishops as "the successors of the apostles" (Vatican Council II, "Decree on the Pastoral Office of Bishops in the Church," no. 8). As Vatican II put it: ". . . the bishops have by divine institution taken the place of the apostles as pastors of the Church, in such wise that whoever listens to them is listening to Christ and whoever despises them despises Christ and him who sent Christ" (Vatican Council II, "Dogmatic Constitution on the Church," no. 20).

Catholicism teaches that these bishops have inherited a threefold power from the apostles:

1. *Teaching*—The bishops have the authority to teach and interpret divine revelation with authority.
2. *Sanctifying*—The bishops have the authority to give spiritual nourishment and to ordain priests or other bishops. They also oversee the administration of the sacraments.
3. *Authority*—The bishops rule the church with spiritual authority granted by Christ to them.

But where did this concept of authority originate? The teaching of papal authority grew out of the church's early relationship to society around it. Linear historical succession to Peter (believed by confessional Roman Catholics to be the first pope) is a matter that may well be debated till the end of the age. What is beyond serious debate is the influence early Roman law and cultural practice had upon the church.

What is clear is this: The early church underwent profound change in the years that followed Emperor Constantine's conversion to Christianity. Over 200 years of intense persecution, usually coming as waves of opposition followed by times of relative peace, had influenced the growth and development of the Christian church under Roman rule. In A.D. 312 Constantine, while preparing for a battle with his political rival Maxentius, professed to see a cross in the midday sun inscribed with the words "In This Sign Conquer." The emperor ordered his soldiers to mark their shields with the sign of the cross. The battle that ensued resulted in complete victory for Constantine. Not long after this success on the battlefield Constantine ordered that Christians no longer be persecuted. This was followed by Constantine showing political favor to the once-hated Christian church.

As a result of this great shift in political fortunes the church began to prosper outwardly. The bishop of Rome was no longer an enemy of the state but a friend. Constantine began to donate monies into the coffers of the church and even declared Sunday, the day of Christian worship, a holiday. Three large basilicas were built in Rome: St. Peter's, St. Paul's, and a third for the bishop himself.

Today the Basilica of St. Peter is located in Vatican City, which is an independent state within the ancient city of Rome. Modern governments recognize the Vatican by sending ambassadors to speak with her on an official basis. (For some time, the United States resisted sending such a representative to the Vatican because of our history of separating church and state. In the 1980s, under the influence of President Ronald Reagan, this policy was changed and the Vatican was finally recognized officially by our government.)

This background helps us understand the key points of the development of papal authority over the centuries.

The Primacy of the Pope

Where exactly did this concept of authority originate? The answer to this question is much debated, but what follows is a serious suggestion based upon the ebb and flow of church tradition.

What can be seen, and this considerably prior to the Middle Ages, is an increasingly unified institutional church organized along lines both juridical (that is, pertaining to the law—in this case the Roman law) and monarchical (that is, following the pattern of a single head, or monarch). An evolution was going on during these centuries that led, by the ninth century, to a church directed by the human authority of a single leader—a pope. The dogma of the papacy gradually developed until it reached its doctrinal apex in Vatican Council I (1870).

The dogma of the papacy actually added to the rupture that took place between the churches of the East (Orthodox Church) and the West (Roman Catholic Church) on July 16, 1054. This division, described accurately by the *Catholic Encyclopedia*, happened "when Cardinal Humbert, the head of a papal delegation in Constantinople, placed a document of excommunication on the altar of Hagia Sophia, the cathedral church of Constantinople." Why was this done? "The official reasons for this were the removal of the filioque [a word meaning "from the Son," which was used to teach that the Holy Spirit proceeded equally from both the Father and the Son] from the Creed; the practice of married clergy and some liturgical errors (for example, the use of leavened bread instead of unleavened bread for the Eucharist)."[1]

This division between the two historic churches has been addressed by recent ecumenical dialogue, especially since 1966 when specific anathemas were lifted by Pope Paul VI and Athenagoras I. But clearly one of the vexing problems that remains between East and West is the papacy of the Roman Catholic Church.

A similar problem existed with regard to the division in the sixteenth century. Luther began his reforming efforts as a loyal subject of the pope. In time he concluded that the whole papal system was unsound. His language, often harsh and offensive to modern readers, must be understood against the backdrop of his times and the way the papacy responded to him as well. Neither Catholic nor Protestant should be proud of the language frequently hurled about in the sixteenth century. Hopefully our remaining vital doctrinal differences can be considered in the future *without* the invectives of the past. Certainly they should be considered without persecution or repression of any sort.

But what exactly is the Roman Catholic doctrine of the papacy? The *Catholic Encyclopedia* again provides help:

> The Bishop of Rome . . . exercises universal jurisdiction over the whole Church as the Vicar of Christ and the Successor of St. Peter. The term "pope" derives from the Latin for "father." . . . In Western Christianity, this term refers to the Roman Pontiff, called His Holiness the Pope, who governs the universal Church as the successor to St. Peter . . . who possesses, "by virtue of his office . . . supreme, full, immediate, and universal ordinary jurisdiction power in the Church (Canon 331)."[2]

This supreme head of the Christian church is said to carry out his pontificate through the offices of bishops, cardinals, and various other offices of the Roman Curia (a body of *official agencies* that assist the pope).

What Is the Biblical Basis for the Papacy?

Roman Catholic apologists never tire of quoting Matthew 16:18-19 when asked to defend the papacy. In this passage Jesus asked Simon Peter who people said He was. Peter answered, "Some say John the Baptist; others say Elijah; and still others, Jeremiah or one of the prophets" (verse 14). Then our Lord asked the disciples, "But what about you? . . . Who do you say I am?" After Peter answered, seemingly for the whole group, "You are the Christ, the Son of the living God" (verse 16), Jesus told Peter that the Father had revealed this truth to him. Then Jesus added this oft-quoted statement: "And I tell you that you are Peter, and on this rock I will build my church, and the gates of Hades will not overcome it. I will give you the keys of the kingdom of heaven; whatever you bind on earth will be bound in heaven, and whatever you loose on earth will be loosed in heaven" (verses 18-19).

The Catholic argument basically goes like this: Peter is the rock in this passage. Christ promises to build His church on the rock. Thus, Peter is the first head, or rock, of the church. The popes (more than 260 historically) who have followed him (supposedly in unbroken succession) are considered heirs of this promise.

Protestants often respond by trying to interpret the reference to the rock in a way that shows why Peter could *not* be the rock in this passage.

Personally, I am in agreement with evangelical New Testament scholar Donald A. Carson, who writes, "If it were not for Protestant reactions against extremes of Roman Catholic interpretation, it is doubtful whether many would have taken 'rock' to be anything or anyone other than Peter."[3] What, then, can we say about Roman Catholic reference to this text in establishing the doctrine of the papacy through Peter as the first pope?

Catholic conclusions from this text suffer from what Carson refers to "as insuperable exegetical and historical problems."[4] For example, after Peter's death his so-called successor would have had authority over a living apostle, John, a prospect that simply cannot be demonstrated. What is actually said in Scripture is that Peter was the first disciple to confess Jesus in this manner, and by this confession his prominence continued into the early years of the church (Acts 1–12). He, along with John, is sent by the other apostles to Samaria (8:14); he is held accountable for his actions by the church in Jerusalem (11:1-18); and he is rebuked by Paul face-to-face (Galatians 2:11-14). Peter is, concludes Carson, first among equals; "and on the foundation of such men (Ephesians 2:20), Jesus built his church. This is precisely why Jesus, toward the close of his earthly ministry, spent so much time with them.

The honor was not earned but stemmed from divine revelation (verse 17) and Jesus' building work (verse 18)."[5]

Modern Catholics will correctly point out that the pope does not speak infallibly on all occasions, and the pope must himself confess personal sin and be redeemed as a sinner. The simple truth is that the doctrine of papal authority, succession, and infallibility is still a major roadblock to meaningful agreement regarding the teachings of the New Testament.

The *Catechism of the Catholic Church*, in speaking of the episcopal college of bishops and the pope, says,

> When Christ instituted the Twelve, "he constituted [them] in the form of a college or permanent assembly, at the head of which he placed Peter, chosen from among them." Just as "by the Lord's institution, St. Peter and the rest of the apostles constitute a single apostolic college, so in like fashion the Roman Pontiff, Peter's successor, and the bishops, the successors of the apostles, are related with and united to one another."
>
> The Pope, Bishop of Rome and Peter's successor, "is the perpetual and visible source and foundation of the unity both of the bishops and of the whole company of the faithful. ... For the Roman Pontiff, by reason of his office as Vicar of Christ, and as pastor of the entire Church has full, supreme, and universal power over the whole Church, a power which he can always exercise unhindered."[6]

Here the Catholic view is stated plainly: Authority was conferred by Christ upon His apostles, Peter being the prince (or supreme head) of them all. From the apostles this same authority is given to the bishops of the church in an *unbroken* line of succession, with supreme authority vested in the Roman pontiff chosen as a successor to Peter since the first century. But a number of nagging questions remain:

1. Was Peter ever in Rome? We don't know for sure, but even if he was it proves nothing. A major problem, however,

is this: When Paul wrote his epistle to the Roman church, why did he address personal greetings to 27 different people but never mention Peter? Strange omission, I believe, if Peter were the supreme head of this flock.

2. Because Peter's name was changed is not proof that he became pope, as has been claimed. Jesus changed the names of other apostles as well (Mark 3:16-17).

3. The Catholic church always lists Peter's name first when it refers to the Twelve. The New Testament does not do this, listing others before Peter on several occasions (for example, John 1:44; Galatians 2:9).

4. Paul spoke of reputed "pillars" of the church in Galatians 2:9 and named, in order, James, Peter, and John. Peter was an important leader for sure, but plainly not the supreme head of them all.

5. Paul, the apostle to the Gentiles, worked independently of Peter and never referred to submitting to Peter (in some sense) as head over all. If anyone qualified as the human leader, it had to be Paul, yet he never claimed any such office for himself. Further, Paul actually rebuked Peter to his face because he stood condemned by his own actions and his hypocritical behavior (Galatians 2:11-14). The unambiguous evidence is this: The headship of the church was not to be found in a single human leader on earth but only in Christ, who reigns from above!

6. Nowhere in any New Testament text is there evidence of the office of pope, and nowhere do we have the model of a person acting as pope. This is a very strange omission if we are to understand that the church is not a true church without this office and the bishops.

What About Infallibility?

Many Roman Catholics are not aware of their own history, especially in terms of theological development and doctrinal formulations. It comes as a surprise, therefore, when they discover that the doctrine of "Papal Infallibility" (clearly delineated and defined) came as late as 1870 at Vatican Council I. Here Pius IX accomplished what he had earlier begun—namely, the strengthening of his leadership over the church. Though this doctrinal conclusion was heatedly debated and widely contested, Vatican Council I ultimately stated that the pope's decisions, when he spoke *ex cathedra* in matters of faith and morals, were "unchangeable in themselves and not because of the consent of the church."[7] The First Vatican Council decreed:

> ...we teach and define as divinely revealed dogma that when the Roman pontiff speaks *ex cathedra,* that is, when, in the exercise of his office as shepherd and teacher of all Christians, in virtue of his supreme apostolic authority, he defines a doctrine concerning faith or morals to be held by the whole church, he possesses, by the divine assistance promised to him in blessed Peter, that infallibility which the divine Redeemer willed his church to enjoy in defining doctrine concerning faith and morals.[8]

It is sometimes argued that Vatican II defined this doctrinal development in such a manner that the essential idea was softened, or altered considerably. This appears not to be the case, however, as the following statement from Vatican II seems to clearly demonstrate:

> The Roman Pontiff, head of the college of bishops, enjoys this infallibility in virtue of his office, when, as supreme pastor and teacher of all the faithful... [he] proclaims in an absolute decision a doctrine pertaining to faith or morals. For that reason his definitions are rightly said to be irreformable by their very nature and not by reason of the assent of the Church, in as much as they were made with the assistance of the Holy Spirit promised to him in the person of the blessed Peter himself; and as a consequence they are

in no way in need of the approval of others, and do not admit of appeal to any other tribunal.[9]

There are several significant problems with this more recent doctrinal development. When the pope issues encyclicals, or other doctrinal statements in written form, are these *ex cathedra*? How do we know what is "from the chair" and what is not? (And what about the 1998 papal declaration regarding "The Great Jubilee of the Year 2000"? Here is a papal document that makes sweeping claims for those who perform certain actions that might result in a plenary indulgence.) Even Catholic scholars continue to debate the meaning of how to apply the idea of infallibility.

The famous nineteenth-century convert to Rome, Cardinal John Henry Newman, actually contested this development in dogma, arguing that historical evidence argued against restricting the authority of the church to the papacy. But Cardinal Newman was a minority voice then, and remains so at the end of the twentieth century.

Vatican Council II (1962–1965) did modify the doctrine of infallibility by saying that the college of bishops *assists* the pope. Whereas the earlier Council had taken a more anti-Protestant stance, Vatican II seemed to address dangers within the Catholic Church itself and tried to reform modern practice. The fact is, collegiality (i.e., the idea that bishops collectively share authority) is still generally interpreted in the light of papal supremacy. *De Ecclesia*, a Vatican II reformist document, states this clearly:

> The college or body of bishops has no authority unless it is simultaneously conceived of in terms of its head, the Roman Pontiff, Peter's successor, and without any lessening of his power of primacy over all, pastors as well as the general faithful. For in virtue of his office, that is, as Vicar of Christ and pastor of the whole Church, the Roman Pontiff has full, supreme, and universal power over the Church. And he can always exercise this power freely.[10]

This same document on the church, which comes from a section dealing with ecumenism and the church's relationship to Protestant churches, adds, "Thus religious submission of the will and mind must be shown in a special way to the authentic teaching authority of the Roman Pontiff, even when he is not speaking ex cathedra."

The Catholic Doctrine of Authority

All Catholic teaching regarding authority in the church and in the life of the faithful centers on the previously mentioned triad of the Bible, tradition, and the magisterium. This is often not understood by evangelicals who speak of ecclesial "cooperation" with Roman Catholic ministries, priests, or churches.

The Catholic concept of tradition is vital to understanding how the Bible must be used and understood. The word *tradition* (from the Latin word for "handing over") refers to the teachings and practices handed down, whether in written or oral form, separately from, but not independently of, Holy Scripture.

The *Catholic Encyclopedia* says,

> Tradition is divided into two areas: (1) Scripture, the essential doctrines of the Church, the major writings and teachings of the Fathers, the liturgical life of the Church, and the living and lived faith of the whole Church down through the centuries; (2) customs, institutions, practices which express the Christian Faith."[12]

The *Catholic Encyclopedia* goes on to say that

> ...the Council of Trent (1546), in distinct opposition to evangelical faith and practice, affirmed "both the Bible and Tradition as divine sources of Christian doctrine." Vatican II states, "It is clear...that, in the supremely wise arrangement of God, sacred Tradition, sacred Scripture and the

> Magisterium of the Church are so connected and associated that one of them cannot stand alone without the others. Working together, each in its own way under the action of the one Holy Spirit, they all contribute effectively to the salvation of souls."[13]

According to the *Catholic Encyclopedia*, the magisterium is "the teaching office of the church." It was established, according to Catholic belief, in order "to safeguard the substance of faith in Jesus Christ" and to prevent the individual from "being left entirely on his own."[14]

It is believed, very simply, that Christ established an apostolic college in His disciples, who, unified with Peter as their head, became the teaching magisterium of the first church. It is further believed that the understanding of this magisterium and its limits, role, and work were ironed out in the centuries that followed, especially at the Council of Trent and Vatican I. The magisterium proclaims the teachings of Christ "infallibly, irreformably and without error" when it follows principles that assure its faithfulness (as defined, of course, by the church).

What all of this means, practically, is that Rome may alter matters that will change how Catholics perceive and experience the life of their church, but fundamental doctrines (such as those we have considered in this book) do not and cannot change. This is what has been meant by the oft-quoted phrase *semper idem* (Latin, "always the same").

In practice the typical Catholic never experiences the magisterium directly. He reads and hears of its deliberations and actions. Where he actually experiences the authority of the church is in the priesthood of his local parish. Here the chain of command comes down to the level of how he or she must actually live and act as a devout Catholic. Here the person receives the sacraments, receives forgiveness for sin, and seeks to know God through his church.

Even at the level of the local parish priest there is a powerful connection to the structure of the Roman Catholic church internationally. That is why we can speak of an American Catholic Church, but ultimately it too is intimately related to the Roman Catholic Church, as centered in the Vatican. Certain American Catholics are prone, at times, to almost lose sight of this reality.

Further, all that is believed and taught at the local parish level is, ultimately, to be related to tradition, the magisterium, and the pope. That is why it is utterly impossible for one priest, or one parish, to be consistently *evangelical* and still be properly related to the Roman Catholic church, at least as defined in its own creeds and practices. Individual Catholic priests and bishops may express personal evangelical views on doctrinal matters, but in reality they cannot remain truly loyal to their church and at the same time embrace *consistently* evangelical views regarding church authority.

The New Testament Pattern

There is a much greater appeal to modern Catholic minds in this doctrine than many evangelicals realize. We live in an age of independence. Often the spirit of our time is the spirit of anarchy. Ours will most likely be known as the age of "personal rights." Christians who observe the spirit of our times often find attractive a church with a supreme pastor who has authority over all matters and to whom we can safely submit ourselves.

Indeed, in every age a tension has existed between submission to one (or several) who has authority over me and my personal responsibility to exercise discernment and make personal decisions based on an authority that is above all present human and ecclesiastical structure. Many evangelicals are members of churches where church leaders (or a single pastor) have become virtual popes in a similar sense.

As an evangelical Christian my reason for rejecting the Catholic doctrine of authority in the papacy and the magisterium (and the more recently developed doctrine of papal infallibility) is not because I desire to foster rebellion, much less willful independence. It is because this doctrine, like so many others that we have observed, is simply *not* grounded in the New Testament. In fact, I believe that this doctrine runs counter to the teaching and spirit of the Scriptures.

The overwhelming majority of New Testament scholars agree that it is debatable whether the New Testament actually presents one uniform pattern of church government. What *is* noticeable, however, when one reads through the New Testament itself, is that there is *development* from Pentecost right through to the pastoral epistles. Let me briefly explain.

Initially, the leadership of the early church was in the hands of the apostles. Catholics and Protestants agree on this. The first division of responsibility and work seems to have come in Acts 6:1-6, when the early church appointed seven men ("full of the Spirit") to care for needs within the local church. Most believe this appointment was the prototype of the office of deacon, which later developed. What is clear is this: The Greek terms for elders, bishops, and pastors are all used interchangeably in the New Testament. They functioned alongside apostles and prophets (and the less-defined person called an "evangelist") for a period of time.

A consistent church structure cannot be easily worked out on the basis of these various terms. What seems clear to most Bible scholars is that these terms are fluid, imprecise, and often used interchangeably. For example, we see an apostle described as an elder (1 Peter 5:1) and one of the seven in Acts 6 is described later as an "evangelist" (Acts 21:8). It also appears that some elders preached while others may not have done so (see 1 Timothy 5:17). And some people preached who were not elders at all (such as Apollos—Acts 18:24-26).

Scottish theologian Donald MacLeod concludes:

> What emerges from the New Testament is not a graduated list of office-bearers with precise designations and clearly defined functions, but clear evidence of three forms of ministry: a ministry of tables (performed by apostles, deacons, and some women); a ministry of oversight and pastoral care (performed by apostles, elders, bishops and pastors); and a ministry of the word (performed by apostles, prophets, evangelists, elders and deacons—and by some with no designation at all).[15]

Summing Up

Martin Luther opposed "enthusiasts" (visionaries, prophets, etc.) in the sixteenth century in much the same way that he countered the papacy. Both, Luther maintained, sought to exercise an authority above and beyond the written Scriptures. Their independence from God's Word was the primary problem. The church does not give us "new birth." It is by the Word of God that we are begotten by the Holy Spirit (see James 1:18; 1 Peter 1:13). Further, we have but one true supreme head and Chief Shepherd of our souls—Jesus Christ the Lord! His infallible teaching is not found in the human creeds and decisions of a fallible church but in the Word of the living God. This is why every great recovery and spiritual awakening in the history of the church has begun with the rediscovery of the power of God in the written Scriptures, not in ecclesiastical structures.

We can and should honestly discuss how a church with a papacy can relate to a church without such. Ultimately the faithful evangelical must follow Scripture in this discussion. And Catholicism's position presently does not allow for a middle ground. Perhaps Catholicism will change this doctrine in the future, but there is no evidence whatsoever that she will. For the evangelical who remains faithful to the New Testament there is no middle ground either. Truth and unity are not served by covering over this major difference; rather, truth is best served by recognizing the supreme headship of Jesus Christ (alone) over the entire universal church.

All human leaders—pastors, deacons, elders—must govern and lead only in a distinctly subservient role as "fellow priests" (see Revelation 1:6; 5:10; 20:6) with all of the people of God. Such leaders are to serve in a spirit of gentleness that honors Christ, the true and only supreme head of the church. And these leaders must serve with derived authority, living totally under the written Scripture and its final authority.

CHAPTER EIGHT

Spiritual Life and Devotion

Nowhere is the difference between evangelical belief and practice more distinct from Catholic belief and practice than in the area of Christian spirituality. Both approaches to the Christian life, as we have seen, are centered on confession of Jesus Christ. Both agree that grace flows from and through Christ as Savior. But Catholicism believes the mystery of Christ's presence in His church makes it possible for the people of God to be given new life through the sacraments, personal devotion, and prayer. Here the mystery of the Catholicism becomes spiritual reality through the church.

In the mystery that is true Catholicism the individual comes to the realization of salvation through a *process* of sanctification that comes about only through faithful participation in the sacraments and personal devotional life. The best simple expression of this can be seen in the modern catechism:

> ...What faith confesses, the sacraments communicate: by the sacraments of rebirth, Christians have become "children of God," "partakers of the divine nature." Coming to see in the faith their new dignity, Christians are called to lead henceforth a life "worthy of the gospel of Christ." They are

> made capable of doing so by the grace of Christ and the gifts of the Spirit, which they receive through the sacraments and through prayer (*Catechism of the Catholic Church,* sect. 1692).

For faithful Catholics, spiritual life comes primarily through the channels offered by the church. This is why salvation is so intimately connected to the life of the church. This understanding of the Christian life can be defined as "the life of grace anchored in the rhythm of the liturgical year's celebration of the mystery of Christ, His mother and His saints; nourished by the food of the Eucharist, sustained by the grace of the other sacraments and deepened by communal participation in the daily public prayer of the Church and the private devotion to which the individual soul is attracted."[1]

Evangelical faith and life, at least confessionally and historically, has been linked much more closely with the Word of God (i.e., the written Scriptures) and the work of the Holy Spirit. As the Word of God is read, taught, preached, and heard, faith is born and it is strengthened by the agency of the Holy Spirit. For this reason, when Catholics visit evangelical churches, they are often surprised at the prominent place the sermon has in worship. For the Catholic the homily is not central, the Mass is. As evangelical theologian Donald Bloesch has observed, "Whereas evangelical Protestantism tends to uphold a theology of the Word of God, the Catholic and Orthodox traditions have generally gravitated toward a theology of the spiritual life."[2]

Evangelicals also give considerable attention to spiritual development and personal devotion to Christ, but in the best of its tradition it has always done this in a manner that subordinates this devotional activity to the revelation of the written Scriptures. Only in recent years has a major shift taken place that has prompted growing numbers of evangelicals to be occupied with a spirituality that is actually more Catholic than evangelical.[3]

The difference between these two traditions, notes Donald Bloesch, is in both emphasis and orientation. Evangelical spiritual exercise is based upon the unmerited grace of God rather than upon human response in the exercise of a particular approach. In Catholic theology, salvation is usually pictured as a joint venture in which we come to God seeking His grace to help us in our endeavor to know Him.

> In evangelical Protestantism grace does more than enable our free will; it liberates our will for faith and service. Grace does not simply bring us the possibility of a salvation yet to be realized; it brings us the reality of a salvation already accomplished. Our role is not to cooperate with God in procuring grace or justification but to celebrate and proclaim a salvation won by Christ alone (*solus Christus*). We are not agents of God's saving work, but witnesses to His saving work. His grace when it first comes to us is irresistible, for it breaks down the resistance of the old nature and in effect implants within us a new nature. The decision of faith is a sign that grace is working for us and in us; it is not the condition for receiving grace.[4]

Mysticism

Christian mysticism, variously debated and defined, is at the very heart of the Catholic mystery. Mysticism is a form of religious practice that seeks *direct* knowledge of God. It generally refers to the type of religious experience through which the believer arrives at a special union of love with God. This experience is generally believed to transcend a knowing that is achieved by the normal powers of mind and reason. Mysticism frequently centers on a desire to experience the "nearness of God" in a state that might be ecstatic. The focus is always on the interior life of the spirit.

The stress of mystical experience is usually on an encounter apart from either Scripture or normal relationships. (In other words, it is highly individualistic.) Emphasis is on the transcendent. Prayer is not understood so much as asking and receiving but as contemplation, often including acts of asceticism that ostensibly promote mystical experience.

Mysticism has often arisen in the history of the Christian church when undue emphasis has been placed upon institutional church life. The reason for this is plain: The mystical way offers opportunity for more direct and personal knowledge of God when He seems distant. Often, debates about creeds and confessions push certain kinds of people into mysticism. An evangelical faith that focuses upon right doctrine, to the exclusion of warm and personal devotion to Jesus Christ, will inevitably produce an arid orthodoxy that repels people who feel deeply about spiritual reality. Some types of Protestant fundamentalism, for example, have produced a sterile affirmation of personal salvation through right mental assent without properly stressing right relationship with the person of Jesus Christ. People who grow up in these circles sometimes rush for any expression of personal faith that can restore serious elements of mystery to their lives. The simple truth is this: When faith is reduced to propositions, or mechanical statements repeated through strong coaching, the end result will often be lifeless faith, regardless of how it originated.

All Christian truth is mystery. We must understand this. Evangelicals often act as if this were not so. (By this I mean that all Christian truth could not be known to humans unless God Himself revealed it to them.) Even though truth can be formulated and explained so that rational minds can respond to it with an informed will, ultimately, God's truth cannot be fully explored or even made palatable to natural minds. The reason for this is the Fall. We not only sin, but we are also fundamentally sinners in every part of our being, including our minds. We are not able to see or fully comprehend and explain God, yet we can state in understandable propositions what God has revealed in Scripture. These revealed truths can be expressed in human language so that truth is communicated to rational beings made in God's image.

Let me illustrate what I mean: The Christian church accepts the doctrine of the Trinity. We believe that God is one God, yet He exists in three persons—the Father, the Son, and the Holy Spirit. We believe this because the Bible reveals it as so, not because our natural minds have rationally discovered it. We cannot adequately explain what the doctrine of the Trinity means, or what it doesn't mean, at least in terms of the questions that remain for us in the face of revelation. We will never be able to explain the triune nature of God so as to satisfy every question. There remains within this important doctrine, simply stated, mystery. Eternity might well reveal fuller elements of the mystery, but one wonders if we shall not still be left with a multitude of questions that have answers which are beyond our human ability to comprehend.

Mysticism is the practice of a kind of faith that believes we can apprehend God *directly* through our subjective experiences, as by intuition. Mysticism believes that the curtain of mystery can be drawn back—to some extent, at least—through a direct experience of the soul with God. The stress in this practice is often on the ways, or stages, of knowing God. Special types of prayer get me into His transcendence more directly; certain practices prepare me to encounter Him in the inner depths of my being. These are part of the mystical way of life.

Evangelical Christianity has sometimes fallen into mysticism, as in the Quaker movement and in much of the modern Charismatic movement. In contrast, historic evangelicalism has stressed the use of the spiritual disciplines as the appointed means for careful response to God's initiatives in Christ. What this means is that we come to God *only* through Christ as our sole Mediator and by the written Scriptures, which are illuminated to our minds by the Holy Spirit.

An example of my point can be seen in the teaching of older, more confessional evangelical churches. Here the stress was on reading the Bible in a spirit of prayerfulness, with meditation included (meditation is neither "repetition" nor "centering" in this tradition). This older evangelicalism does not stress "surrendering my inner faculties" to the light of God through an experience of irrational love. Perhaps the best and certainly the most balanced evangelical teaching on this subject can be seen in the English Puritans. With them, confessional Christianity was generally blended with the disciplines of practical godliness in a marvelous way.

Roman Catholicism has always welcomed mysticism far more openly than evangelicalism. One needs only recount the claims of the saints through the ages—their visions and apparitions, the special visitations of angels, the place of Mary, and even of the mystical Christ of visionary encounter. Closely associated with all this mystical practice are two important areas of Catholic devotion that we will consider in this chapter.

The Sacramentals

As we have already seen, the Catholic Church teaches that grace is conveyed to faithful people through the sacraments. Beyond this she has variously taught that there are both things and actions which, when blessed by the church, become sacramentals, or "sacred signs." These are believed to bear a certain likeness to the sacraments. In them spiritual effects are signified and obtained by the intercession of the church.[5]

These sacramentals include objects such as holy water, scapulars (two pieces of cloth suspended on the shoulders), medals, and rosaries. Other sacramentals may include actions, such as blessings and exorcisms. Sacramentals can be changed by the church, since it is the church which institutes them. In distinction, it is believed that the seven sacraments were instituted by Christ and thus are unchangeable.

In a most interesting and candid statement, the *Catholic Encyclopedia* acknowledges that "Sacramentals differ from sacraments . . . in the manner of imparting grace (a sacrament imparts grace in virtue of the rite itself, while the grace of the sacramentals depends on the dispositions of the recipient and the intercession of the Church.) The number of sacramentals is variable.[6]

Here we encounter something that is again inconsistent with the practice revealed in the New Testament itself. According to Catholic teaching, sacramentals have no power in themselves, yet they *convey grace* if the one who uses them has a right heart, or believing disposition. What we have here is a connection of external objects and actions with a mystical understanding of faith that is inherent in the Catholic mystery itself.

I am afraid that in actual practice this subtle distinction is lost on many of my Catholic friends. Ordinary devout Catholics seem to attribute huge importance to the sacramentals in their daily devotion. One reason for this is the relationship of mystical experience to the sacramentals. The sacramentals make a wonderful provision for mystical experience through something tangible, something ordinary. It allows the mystical experience to be readily available to the devout common person. Further, some of the statements about the value of sacramentals from the history of Catholicism add to the mystique of this. Here are a few illustrations of what I mean.

Pope Leo X wrote, "The rosary has been established against the dangers which threaten the world." Pope Pius V said, "By the rosary the darkness of heresy has been dispelled, and the light of the Catholic faith shines out in all its brilliance." Popes Clement VII and Clement X declared that all who wore the scapular

> ...participated in a special manner in the fruit of all the good done throughout the whole Catholic Church.... The associates (wearers) of this scapular have received the promise...to be adopted by the Blessed Virgin as her favorite and privileged children, and to enjoy during life her special protection both of soul and body... as she promised to St. Simon Stock: "He who dies with this scapular shall not suffer eternal fire."[7]

Devotion to Mary

There can be no question that the place of Mary in Roman Catholic doctrine and practice is another unique difference between evangelical faith and Catholicism. Significant areas of Catholic devotion and practice are powerfully connected to Mary. The views one encounters range from a genuine appreciation of Mary as the humble handmaiden of the Lord and the mother of Christ to strong, clear ascriptions of near-divinity to her.

Before we embark on a brief survey of Catholic teaching on Mary, we need to understand something about the Catholic Church that has not been clearly stated previously. According to Catholic doctrine, the church is Jesus Christ "available." In its *Dogmatic Constitution on the Church*, Vatican II speaks of the mystery of the church first. As *Lumen Gentium* puts it, the holy catholic and apostolic church "subsists in the Catholic Church, which is governed by the successor of Peter and by the bishops in union with this successor." In this conception the church exists "alongside of the person of Christ."[8]

Rome views itself as "one interlocked reality which is comprised of a divine and a human element."[9] Because of this there is a synthesis of human and divine elements in Roman Catholic thought that baffles evangelicals. The great mystery of the church, according to this teaching, is that it is an actual extension of Christ's incarnation throughout the world. As noted in an extremely useful little volume, "Since Mary is a picture of the church, in exalting Mary, the Roman Catholic Church exalts itself."[10]

The place of Mary in Roman Catholic devotion is similar to the relationship of the Catholic worshiper to the saints in general. Following the Second Lateran Council (A.D. 787), Rome made a distinction between veneration due to the saints and the worship due only to God. As early as this ancient Lateran Council Mary was believed to be in a special class beyond all the saints of the church. To her the believer rendered higher veneration, placing her above all other saints but a little lower than God.

This devotion to Mary has occupied an important place in the mystical practice of Catholics for centuries. Evangelicals are generally quite ignorant of how profoundly this experience of devotion to Mary affects their Catholic friends. An example of what I mean can be seen, and felt, in the clearly articulated expression of a friend who was a cradle Catholic for over thirty years. He practiced the Catholic mystery through profound devotion and faith. He writes of his past struggles, which eventually brought him to evangelical faith and practice:

> "Mary, conceived without sin, to thee do I have recourse." To the one drawn by the thought of a loving mother's comfort and protection, allow the Scriptures to speak for the heart of God: "Can a mother forget the baby at her breast and have no compassion on the child she has borne? Though she may forget, I will not forget you! See, I have engraved you on the palms of My hands" (Isaiah 49:15,16). Mary should be emulated for her childlike faith and for her love of God and Scripture (as revealed in her beautiful Magnificat). Mary should be revered by evangelicals and Catholics alike, for she was singled out in human history by our sovereign God to bear and raise the Messianic hope of Israel and the world. However, to elevate her to the status of "Co-Redemptrix," "Mediatrix of all graces," and the like shows no real honor to her, and ultimately and tragically,

robs both the Father and the Son of their glory and theirs alone in the redemption of God's elect.

The Mary of the New Testament is not revealed as the "Queen of Heaven," and she would not gladly receive the hyper-veneration of millions whose sights should be on Christ alone. Being the center of spiritual devotion for multitudes worldwide would grieve the heart of the woman who would most likely say, in all humility, "Do whatever He [Jesus] tells you." Learn as I, by God's grace, did: honor Mary, model her virtues, but trust in Christ and in Him alone.

It is a well-established fact that Marian rituals and festivals grew as the early church expanded. It also would appear that the growth of this veneration was partly aimed at countering vestigial goddess worship present in parts of Europe. The church in the fourth century began to emphasize a cult of Mary. Over the years that followed, doctrines gradually developed around devotion to the mother of our Lord. Some of these were officially accepted by the church.

At the Council of Trent (1545–1563), due to reaction against Protestant opposition to much of this growing emphasis, Mary's sinlessness and perpetual virginity were affirmed by the church as official dogma. Two other important doctrinal developments were later added. First, the Immaculate Conception, which refers to the teaching that Mary was conceived without original sin, was accepted. This dogma was recognized by the church only in 1854. As late as 1950 the Catholic Church officially accepted the dogma of Mary's Assumption, meaning that she was assumed, body and soul, into heaven.

The non-Catholic reader needs to understand that these dogmas are "doctrines of faith," which means *they must be believed* by devout and faithful Catholics. If you reject these newer doctrines as unscriptural, then you must also come to grips with this simple fact—you have rejected your church because you have rejected its authority to develop, define, and interpret dogma for the faithful.

Of all the Catholic teachings that surround the veneration of Mary, only the doctrine of the Virgin Birth is plainly taught in the New Testament itself. As noted previously (chapter 7), the answer to the question "Who speaks for God?" remains at the very center of the canyon of difference that still exists between evangelical faith and Catholicism. The Catholic Church appeals to the magisterium and the continuation of the incarnate ministry of Jesus in and through the church; thus it adds these teachings *without* clear biblical warrant.

In the early centuries of the church Mary was defined as "the Mother of God" because of debates that surrounded the nature of Christ Himself. If He were indeed God in human flesh and Mary was His mother, then she was, logically, the Mother of God. So far so good—except that evangelicals would rather stay with the language of the biblical text and say that Mary was "the mother of Jesus," or "the mother of our Lord." Why this particular insistence? Because, though she was the *human* mother of the man Jesus, she was not *the mother of God* in the sense of somehow *generating* His divinity or in having an authority equal to His.

It is important that we understand the Catholic respect for Mary properly. In the Catholic mystery Mary is not only the mother of Christ, she is the mother of the *entire* church. The reasoning goes like this: When Jesus was on the cross He named Mary as the mother of St. John, thus confirming her spiritual motherhood for all who have life in Himself since John, it is reasoned, represented the whole body of faithful believers (John 19:25-27). Mary's close association with the church is now symbolized in the Mass, since she mystically became one with His sufferings while He was on the cross. She is also symbolized in baptism, since the church, by bringing souls to life in Christ through baptism, joins Mary in her consent to the incarnation.

In this paradigm, Mary literally becomes the model of the faithful. Since her life was fully devoted to Christ, she is considered an inspiration for all who believe. Priests and nuns say that they draw strength from her because their calling is similar to that given to her. Families see in Mary the witness of a holy family and say that they draw personal help from her. All see in her both strength and courage, thus experiencing something of her life in them.

Mary has been given numerous titles that reflect the basic beliefs held regarding her. These include:

1. Our Blessed Mother. This stresses her motherly concern for believers and her special concern for their holiness. It is a title of deep affection.
2. Ever Virgin. This signifies her perpetual virginity, a doctrine the church affirms. It demonstrates her complete dedication to God's redemptive plan by her continual virginity.
3. Queen of Heaven. This title reflects the church's belief that she reflects the image for the church of the full flowering of Christ's redemption. She is an emblem of hope for all the faithful. This title also celebrates another distinct Catholic dogma—namely, that Mary was assumed bodily into heaven.
4. The New Eve. We are reminded by this title that Mary was free of original sin, according to Catholic dogma, through the immaculate conception. This emphasizes her obedience to God's will, helping to bring us redemption from the evil caused by the first Eve's disobedience.
5. *Theotokos*. This refers to the Greek word for "Mother of God." It expresses, in Marian theology, the mystery of God made human flesh. It displays the unique closeness of Mary to Christ, the foundation and source of all her other glories.
6. Mediatrix. A title that suggests Mary plays an active—though subordinate—role in our salvation. It also

reminds Catholics of the belief that Mary will intercede for them.

As the mother of Christ it is believed that Mary is a model of perfection because she was perfectly devoted to Christ's redemptive mission. Knowing this truth, it is affirmed, can improve relationships with both Christ and other people. This is done with Christ by gaining from Mary a better understanding how to love and serve others. With other people, this is gained by following her example. The Blessed Virgin is believed to be like a window through which the light of Christ falls upon us. This holy window helps us to grow in faith, hope, and love. Said Pope Paul VI, "The person who encounters Mary cannot but encounter Christ likewise." And John Paul II is well known for his particular devotion to Mary.

Marian devotion takes several forms. Through prayer the devout Catholic seeks to commune with Mary, as well as with the other members of the mystical body of Christ. These prayers may include: 1) veneration—wherein reverence is expressed for Mary's unique holiness; 2) invocation—wherein Mary is petitioned to intercede for us and help us in our weaknesses and trials; 3) imitation—wherein the faithful meditate on the qualities of the life of the Blessed Virgin, who is a model of perfect responsiveness to God.

The restored church calendar, approved by Vatican II, commemorates Christ's mother throughout the church year. There are four Great Solemnities of the Blessed Virgin, which are times to remember various doctrines about Mary. There are also five feasts that celebrate several truths revealed about Mary in Holy Scripture.

By contrast, here's what the New Testament actually says about Mary:

1. Those who honor Mary best honor her son directly, not Mary (see Luke 1:48; 11:27-28). And those who truly honor her hear the word of Jesus and obey it (see John 2:5).

2. In absolutely no sense does Mary contribute anything to our salvation, according to the angelic announcement to Mary in Matthew 1:21: "You shall call His name Jesus, for it is *He* who will save His people from their sins" (NASB).

3. Mary acknowledged that Jesus was her Savior and understood her own role in this simply: "Behold, the bondslave of the Lord; be it done to me according to your word" (Luke 1:38 NASB). And in the passage commonly called "The Magnificat of Mary," she praises God by saying, "My spirit has rejoiced in God my Savior" (verse 47 NASB). Mary plainly sees Jesus as *her Redeemer*; thus she must have been a sinner like any other mortal human. Only sinners need a Redeemer. Further, she knew her role was to be the Lord's bondslave, not to share *directly* in redemption in any way.

4. Jesus taught with equal plainness: "I am the way and the truth and the life. No one comes to the Father except through me" (John 14:6). All human cooperation in salvation is a matter of giving men and women the truth of Christ and allowing Him, by the Holy Spirit, to bring them to Jesus alone! It is Jesus who ushers believers into the presence of His Father. His mother is never said to have any role in this redeeming process at all.

5. Not one reference to Mary as the "Queen of Heaven" or the "Queen of Mercy" is found anywhere in the New Testament.

Serious Catholic exegesis of the Greek texts of Matthew and Luke reveal that at one level there remains a possibility for renewed biblical appreciation for the place of Mary. At the same time, these newer exegetes do not accept all the centuries-long veneration that goes quite far beyond the biblical account itself. Both Joseph Fitzmyer, as well as the late Raymond Brown, hold views of the biblical text that are much closer to those held by serious evangelical scholars![11]

In spite of the simple texts we have in Scripture and the present renewal in Catholic exegesis, Pope John Paul II, in his encyclical *Redemptor Hominis*, titled the last chapter "The Mother in Whom We Trust." In this document Mary is given an extremely prominent place in the history of salvation: "We who form today's generation of disciples of Christ all wish to unite ourselves with her in a special way.... We believe that nobody else can bring us as Mary can into the divine and human dimension of mystery."[12]

Evangelicals may well have overreacted by ignoring Mary's sterling character as revealed in the pages of Scripture. She is, no doubt, a model to all of us of a humble servant of the Lord, highly favored by God because of her submissive spirit. In a time when men and women alike need a Christian role model, Mary is a wonderful example of simple trust in the Father's bestowal and grace.

The Saints

Catholic spiritual practice also includes the mystery of "the communion of the saints." The *Catholic Encyclopedia* says, "Paul uses this word [saints] for Christians in general (Col. 1:2). Strictly speaking, saints are people whose lives were notable for holiness and heroic virtue."[13] Saints are made such through the church's officially declaring them saints by a process called beatification and canonization. These saints are in heaven and can be invoked, with proper devotion, to intercede for us sinners on earth.

Vatican II says that saints are those who are joined to God in "sharing forever a life that is divine and free from all decay." Saints, furthermore, "have found true life with God"; thus they "share in his life and glory."

The veneration of saints is an important part of the Catholic mystery. A visit to any local Catholic church, cathedral, or shrine will reveal this point.

But once again, a straightforward reading of the New Testament reveals that the word *saint* is never used in this way at all. In the New Testament the word is consistently used as a synonym for all of those who truly believe in Christ. For example, Paul writes that the Ephesian believers are to "always keep on praying for all the saints" (Ephesians 6:18). And the last book of the New Testament describes the prayers of all those gathered around the throne of Christ as "the prayers of the saints" (Revelation 5:8). Verse after verse in Scripture demonstrates that *saint* is a synonym for all true Christian believers (see also Romans 8:27; Ephesians 1:18; Revelation 19:8).

What's more, the mysticism that leads to praying through the saints or invoking their aid has no biblical warrant. The only biblical explanation sometimes offered is that we all ask other people to pray for us (intercession), thus invoking their help on our behalf. But surely there is big difference between asking a friend to intercede for me in prayer, a practice revealed and clearly taught in the New Testament, and invoking the meritorious aid of additional mediatorial helpers (the saints and Mary), who are said to appeal to the glorified Christ on our behalf.

The question the biblical Christian must ask is this: "Can Christ understand my struggles, fully identify with me in all of them, and adequately appeal to His Father on my behalf?" The answer found in Scripture is that He, and He alone, can help me (see Hebrews 2:18; 4:15-16; 7:25). He is the High Priest for all who believe. Why would I need any other aid in heaven if the man at God's right hand is none other than Christ Jesus? Why would I appeal to *lesser* help when all I need is in the greater help of His own person and work?

Once again, the emphasis upon merit, experienced through mysticism, comes to the fore. Evangelical faith, by contrast, is satisfied with Christ alone, through grace alone, by faith alone.

Summing Up

The place that Mary and the saints have had in Catholic practice clearly goes beyond the teaching of the New Testament. And in recent years, mystical interest in the saints has been on the rise. Since the declaration of Mary's assumption into heaven in 1950, Mary has been increasingly the object of much adoration and love in the Catholic Church. Older Catholic catechisms spoke of her role as that of a "mediatrix." Such language is not acceptable in light of the apostle Paul's teaching in 1 Timothy 2:5: "There is one God and one mediator between God and men, the man Jesus Christ." Until the language of redemption is removed from references to Mary, evangelicals will never accept this devotion, which plainly has immense importance in the practical life of multitudes of Catholics.

The supposed appearance of Mary at Medjugorje (to six village children) in 1981 has caused millions of pilgrims to visit this site in eastern Europe. Though the Vatican is slow to endorse this visitation, the miracles that have been associated with it tend to encourage implied endorsement in many ways. Father Giuseppe Besutti, a professor at Rome's Pontifical Marianum School, commented, "The church itself is founded on an apparition—that of Christ resurrected."[14] To say the least this kind of language is bizarre, if not an outright attack upon the *singularity* of Christ's unique bodily resurrection from the grave.

The rise of miraculous claims associated with Mary and ardent devotion to her is noticeable, and not just in the underdeveloped poorer countries of the world. Even the Vatican acknowledges a worldwide rise in claims of "pseudo-mysticism, presumed apparitions, visions and messages" associated with Mary. One expert on Marian phenomena, a French theologian named René Laurentin, said in 1990 that there had been more than 200 such events since 1930. Most are viewed skeptically in official circles, yet in the past 160 years the Catholic Church has authenticated 14 apparitions as "worthy of pious belief."

What this means, in essence, is that Catholics are free to believe or disbelieve as they wish. Yet multitudes of worshipers seek apparitions and visions, longing for some mystical encounter with God. A Madonna statue weeps, a Long Island grandmother hears Mary speak to her and relates the messages, icons cry, and Christ "appears" miraculously on garage doors, water towers, and even on a tortilla shell."[15] In 1993 a suburban Virginia priest even experienced bleeding from his wrists. Consequently, the stigmata of previous centuries are again a matter for the practical spiritual agenda of multitudes.[16]

Church officials may be slow to respond to some of this, knowing the dangers associated with definitive response, but they still encourage this preoccupation. Even John Paul II, who has withheld official comment, is quoted as "having made generally supportive statements privately."[17]

The real problem, which we have seen again and again, is that the Catholic Church's doctrine of Scripture allows this evolution of dogma to take place. This fosters the elevation of Mary to the place of adoration. It also allows for the growth of other related practices that fit comfortably into an excessively mystical spirituality. These practices include veneration offered to certain relics that are professed to have a direct connection with Jesus and Mary–such as pieces of wood from the cross of Christ, a vial of Mary's milk, and so on. In the time of the Reformation the inventory of relics that existed in the church was immense. Evangelicals believe that the sixteenth-century Reformer John Calvin correctly attacked this as the enemy of the gospel of sovereign grace.

I am personally convinced that this type of reverence for Mary, the saints, and relics will never go away unless Catholics more carefully conform their faith and practice to the clear teachings of the New Testament. This means that they will have to give up the type of mysticism that prompts such devotion in the first place. This is not easy, as we have noted, for such mysticism is at the very heart of the Catholic mystery itself.

As confessed so pointedly by the Hebrew prophet Isaiah, "To the Law and to the testimony! If they do not speak according to this word, they have no light of dawn [or spiritual light]" (Isaiah 8:20). If we refuse the more certain word of prophecy given to us in the Scriptures (2 Peter 1:19-21), we will repeatedly land in the depths of a mysticism that will swallow up true faith in Christ alone. We must seek guidance from God, but the mystical way confuses two matters—*how* we get God's guidance, and *where* we get it. May God's Spirit be pleased to lead you to search "the Scriptures . . . to see whether these things [are] so" (Acts 17:11, NASB).

CHAPTER NINE

Death and the Life to Come

In the face of the grim reality of death, the Christian faith has always offered a profound hope to those who believe the gospel. The apostle Paul wrote to the church in Corinth, "Death has been swallowed up in victory. Where, O death, is your victory? Where, O death, is your sting?" (1 Corinthians 15:54-55).

Christ continually encouraged His own disciples regarding their hope of life beyond the grave. An example is in John 14:1-4:

> Do not let your hearts be troubled. Trust in God; trust also in me. In my Father's house are many rooms; if it were not so, I would have told you. I am going there to prepare a place for you. And if I go and prepare a place for you, I will come back and take you to be with me that you also may be where I am. You know the way to the place where I am going.

The gospel of Christ is concerned with much more than this present life. Its hope reaches beyond the grave, or its message is simply a hoax.

Both Catholics and evangelicals are concerned with life beyond the grave. Both have much to say doctrinally about this crucial subject, but what is said varies considerably.

Extreme Unction, or Holy Anointing

As we saw in chapter 6, one of the sacraments that Rome practices is anointing, or what Vatican II called "extreme unction." The Council of Trent pronounced an anathema upon those who deny that this sacrament is one truly instituted by Christ.

The Catholic argument is that Jesus had power over sickness, and the Gospels show how He gave that power to His apostles. Mark wrote that the apostles "drove out many demons and anointed many sick people with oil and healed them" (Mark 6:13). The epistle of James indicates that the practice of anointing the sick continued in the early church community (see James 5:14-15). Few references to this practice can be found in the early church Fathers. One reference in Hippolytus says, "This oil . . . may give strength to all that taste of it and health to all that use it."[1]

It was not until the fifth century that Pope Leo I (d. 461) indicated a developed tradition and a new understanding when he wrote to Bishop Decentius. In explaining the James 5 passage, this pope made several points:

1. The bishop alone has the right to consecrate the oil.
2. In the absence of the bishop, the priest may anoint the sick person, and this anointing is sacramental.
3. The oil may also be used by lay persons for a nonsacramental anointing. (When we come to the Middle Ages the rise of references to healing the sick through this sacrament increase dramatically.)[2]

In the East the rite became more closely associated with a person who was dying and the forgiveness of sins before death. Because of this emphasis the practice was looked upon as final and was associated with *dying penance*. Bokenkotter observes that the West also followed this practice: "Those who received the sacrament and by chance recovered were bound by the ancient canons to severe practices such as abstaining from all marital relations, etc. Thus the anointing came to be called extreme unction."[3] Vatican II sought to recover this early practice and to connect it with the healing of the sick.

The modern priest is encouraged to confer this sacrament in a way that invites the sick person, and those present, to share fully in a service of readings and prayers while the priest counsels and assists the sick person and his or her relatives and friends. The purpose is "to comfort them and help them respond with faith and trust to the mystery of suffering and death."[4]

Along with this sacrament we come to another death-related ritual that for centuries has been a Catholic practice. I refer to the wearing of the scapular. The scapular is two pieces of brown cloth suspended on the shoulders. It is an attenuated version of the Carmelite scapular that, according to tradition, was granted by the Virgin to Simon Stock, a thirteenth-century English monk, as a sign of his order. A Carmelite publication wrote that this scapular (to be worn by Catholic soldiers in military service) carried a picture of Mary, Joseph, and St. Simon Stock with the words "Whoever lies clothed in this scapular shall not suffer eternal fire."[5]

Why This Approach to Death?

In spite of these extensive preparations for death, why is death still viewed by many Catholics as something other than a hopeful entry into heaven? The evangelical, in contrast, reads the New Testament and finds definite assurance that he or she will enter heaven at the moment of death.

As previously noted, traditional Catholic theology and practice is given over to structuring, rationalizing, and preparing for grace. There is a strong strain of legalism in all of this. Christ's death, in Catholic thought, removes the guilt and corruption of original sin for those baptized. But this is only a "first" justification. It must be followed by a "second," which is based on love working out of the heart. The devout soul, especially if it is the soul of an earnest and well-taught person, is left with perplexing questions that continually gnaw at the heart:

- "Have I really done enough?"
- "When I demonstrated love and charity, was my motive really right before God?"
- "How can I *really* know if God truly accepts my way of living?"

For most Catholics these questions are common. They are pondered regularly, and with much uncertainty regarding the final destiny of their soul after death. However, the person who sincerely ponders the question of life after death will not find questions like these in the New Testament. What he will find are words such as these:

> We are always confident and know that as long as we are at home in the body we are away from the Lord. We live by faith, not by sight. We are confident, I say, and would prefer to be away from the body and at home with the Lord (2 Corinthians 5:6-8).
>
> I am torn between the two [i.e., life and death]: I desire to depart and be with Christ, which is better by far; but it is more necessary for you that I remain in the body (Philippians 1:23-24).

But in the mind of the devout Catholic, there is little hope of *immediate* entry into the Lord's presence in heaven upon death. Although purgatory (or "The Divine Waiting Room" as one author calls it) may not be a desired goal, it is the hoped-for reality of most faithful Catholics. According to Catholic dogma, those who die in mortal sin, in a state of impenitence, go directly to hell. Those who die in a state of *perfect holiness* enter heaven. To this class belong martyrs, whose blood serves for final purification. In practice, according to the Catholic view, the number of people who enter heaven immediately is very small.

The personal impact of this doctrine upon the devout Catholic is not easily understood by most evangelicals. Consider how one former Catholic understood the attraction of this mystery of life after death:

> In the lower sanctuary of the Roman Catholic Church I had attended since childhood stood a statue of the Virgin Mary holding the infant Jesus while descending into purgatory to rescue the "poor souls" in torment. There was Mary, resplendent, reaching out to men and women engulfed in flames, whose faces were contorted by the pain and anguish of purgatorial sufferings. In desperation, each one reached out to Mary, looking upon her to release them from the flames of torment and bring them to heaven. With pity I would often look intently at the pain on their faces and the helpless arms stretching out to touch Mary, even as the flames surrounded them. I was told by the parochial school nuns, who were my teachers, to pray for souls in purgatory so that they might enter heaven where they would then pray for me. So, as a young boy, I would often find myself before that statue, kneeling, lighting votive candles, and offering "Hail Marys" for the departed souls who were on their journey home to heaven.
>
> Only many years later, after much study of the New Testament, as a man in my thirties, did I come to realize how unbiblical this dogma really was. This actually proved to be a real turning point in my spiritual life.

The *Catechism of the Catholic Church* is quite instructive when it says:

> The Christian who unites his own death to that of Jesus views it as a step towards him and an entrance into everlasting life. When the Church for the last time speaks Christ's words of pardon and absolution over the dying Christian, seals him for the last time with a strengthening anointing, and gives him Christ in viaticum as nourishment for the journey, she speaks with gentle assurance.[6]

The phrase "gives him Christ in viaticum" means to give Christ in the Eucharist as preparation for the dying journey.

This sounds hopeful at first glance. On the surface I think that it is, but the hard reality is this: it leaves the devout Catholic with great doubt and fear. The *Catechism* even speaks a few words later of death bringing a person into "the blessedness of heaven . . . immediately" if they are in grace. But, it should be noted, the words preceding "immediately" are "through a purification." We are left here with a huge problem. Most of those who die in grace are simply not adequately "purified" to enter heaven immediately. They need *further purification*. This further purification must take place in purgatory, where "final purification" is believed to occur.

The Basis for the Teaching

What is the basis for this doctrine? The *Catechism* accurately says, "The Church formulated her doctrine of faith on purgatory especially at the Councils of Florence and Trent. The tradition of the Church, by reference to certain texts of Scripture, speaks of a cleansing fire."[7] The Church's practice makes reference to some scripture texts that should be carefully studied: 1 Corinthians 3:15; 1 Peter 1:7; and 1 Peter 3:19.

To say the least, the concept of purgatory is not explicitly stated in these verses. The passage in 1 Corinthians is addressed to those who "build" the church. The simple fact stated here is that these individuals will face a stricter judgment regarding the quality of the materials they used in building their ministry. The first passage in 1 Peter clearly refers to *present* trials which prove our faith genuine. The other passage in 1 Peter makes a contrast between Noah's day and Christ's day in terms of judgment. The best suggestion, I believe, is that a parallel exists here—Noah preached, people disobeyed, and they were judged; Christ preached, people rejected, and they were rejected. Further, the spirits in prison who were preached to were most likely those to whom Christ preached *through Noah* in his ancient time. Regardless of how we solve the admitted difficulties of this problematic passage, there is no *clear* reference to purgatory here.

Further reference is made by Catholic teaching to the apocryphal book of 2 Maccabees: "Therefore [Judas Maccabeus] made atonement for the dead, that they might be delivered from their sin." With this the *Catechism* also encourages prayers for the dead made explicitly at the Eucharistic sacrifice (that is, in the Mass). The *Catechism* sums up this doctrine in one short paragraph under the section "In Brief": "Those who die in God's grace and friendship imperfectly purified, although they are assured of their eternal salvation, undergo a purification after death, so as to achieve the holiness necessary to enter the joy of God."[8]

Alongside the Catholic doctrine of purgatory we find the idea of a treasury of merit as well. This treasury contains the excess merits, or good works, of the saints throughout the ages. It is important to see that in Catholic teaching, it is *not* Christ's merits *alone* that save believers, but Christ's merits plus that of all others who have believed in Him. The Catholic document *Indulgentiarum Doctrina* states this very clearly:

> This treasury includes as well the prayers and good works of the Blessed Virgin Mary. They are truly immense, unfathomable, and even pristine in their value before God. In the treasury, too, are the prayers and good works of all the saints, all those who have followed in the footsteps of Christ the Lord and by his grace made their lives holy and carried out the mission the Father entrusted to them. In this way they attained their own salvation and at the same time cooperated in saving their brothers in the unity of the Mystical Body.

According to this way of thinking, salvation is truly a "self-help" project. It is a project wherein the grace of God gives us divine assistance but we genuinely contribute something to our salvation. And, through our actions, we can also help save others.

An Evangelical Response

How does the evangelical who believes Scripture alone is God's authority, and not the Councils of the Church, respond to a doctrine such as this? Evangelicals stress the perfection, finality, and completion of Christ's once-for-all sacrifice at Calvary. They respond with hope-filled words like these:

> Now there have been many of those priests, since death prevented them from continuing in office; but because Jesus lives forever, he has a permanent priesthood. Therefore he is able to save completely those who come to God through him, because he always lives to intercede for them.
>
> Such a high priest meets our need—one who is holy, blameless, pure, set apart from sinners, exalted above the heavens. Unlike the other high priests, he does not need to offer sacrifices day after day, first for his own sins, and then for the sins of the people. He sacrificed for their sins once for all when he offered himself (Hebrews 7:23-27).
>
> Therefore it was necessary for the copies of the things in the heavens to be cleansed with these, but the heavenly things themselves with better sacrifices than these. For Christ did not enter a holy place made with hands, a mere copy of the true one, but into heaven itself, now to appear in the presence of God for us; nor was it that He would offer Himself often, as the high priest enters the holy place year by year with blood not his own. Otherwise, He would have needed to suffer often since the foundation of the world; but now once at the consummation of the ages He has been manifested to put away sin by the sacrifice of Himself. And inasmuch as it is appointed for men to die once and after this comes judgment, so Christ also, having been offered once to bear the sins of many, shall appear a second time for salvation without reference to sin, to those who eagerly await Him (Hebrews 9:23-28 NASB).

Christ's death met the perfect demands of the violated law of God. All who truly trust in Him alone to save them will enter into heaven not because they have been purified over and over again, but because of the one-time final sacrifice of Christ. To teach otherwise, I submit, is to suggest that Christ's death is not adequate enough to save those who entrust themselves to Him alone.

Further, if sin has been paid for, to pay for it again—in ourselves or in a place called purgatory—is to pay twice for something already bought with the perfect blood of Christ, our High Priest. This means that the atonement of Christ was either not perfect, as the Bible clearly denies, or that God is not just, thus judging the sin twice. The evangelical would say, further, that "the blood of Jesus, his Son, purifies us from *all* sin" (1 John 1:7, emphasis added). How can further purging be needed when Paul says, "God presented him as a sacrifice of atonement, through faith in his blood" (Romans 3:25)? Has Christ's atonement for those who believe in the Son somehow been voided now? No, for the Father has accepted Christ's perfect sacrifice. Furthermore, Paul concludes that through faith in Christ "there is now no condemnation for those who are in Christ Jesus" (Romans 8:1). The only logical deduction that can be drawn from such a statement is this: Purgatory and further cleansing cannot possibly be necessary if the death of Christ truly cleanses us in such a manner that we are brought into a state, *before* death, of being no longer condemned. This is truly good news, isn't it?

For the Catholic, death is *truly* the moment of truth. They cannot know their eternal destiny until then. To them, life is a test. To pass the test is the goal. But no one can really know for sure whether or not they have passed this test until they stand before the Creator. Will I go to purgatory? Will I be rejected, having failed the test altogether? And finally, at the end of the ages, is another judgment, this time a more general one. It is here, they believe, that we will find out the magnitude of our glory in heaven (if we have been granted entrance) or the degree of our torment in hell (if we have been rejected). This approach to death and the life to come definitely does not instill confidence and peace in the souls of devout followers.

Summing Up

This knowledge about one's eternal destiny was a central issue for the evangelical Reformers. It is still a major issue for evangelical Christians who follow the New Testament. It's referred to as the doctrine of assurance: How can I know that I am redeemed and that I will *definitely* go to heaven when I die?

For the devout Catholic the doctrine of assurance is tenuous at best, if not totally nonexistent. You receive the sacraments of your church. You strive to avoid mortal sin. If you fail, you immediately confess your failure. You realize that venial sin is another matter, and you continually labor under its weight. You hope to increase your experience of the grace of God in the mystery which is your church. You are offered comfort in several ways. You pray the rosary, perhaps attend a Bible study, and even give of your wealth to charity and your church. But you are still plagued by the uncertainty of what will happen when you die. Will God accept me into heaven immediately? Or will he reject me? Only when you have a clear answer to this question will you ever know real peace with God in your soul.

The Catholic mystery, then, leaves the devout with little or no assurance. This must be understood in the fullest sense of what is actually taught within Catholic tradition and dogma. In *A Catechism for Adults*, a popularly used teaching tool since Vatican II, Father William J. Cogan asks and answers the central question:

> *Question:* What is necessary to be saved?
>
> *Answer:* You have to be brought into spiritual contact with that saving death of Jesus by faith and Baptism and loyal

> membership in His Church, by love of God and neighbor proved by obedience to His commandments, by the other Sacraments especially Holy Communion, by prayer and good works and by final perseverance, that is, preserving God's friendship and grace until death.[9]

The Council of Trent very clearly articulated the historical tradition of Catholic dogma by stating it this way: "If anyone says that the justice revealed is not preserved and also not increased before God through good works, but that those works are merely the fruits and signs of justification obtained, but not the cause of its increase, let him be anathema" (Session vi, canon 24).

I still recall how stunned I was when, as a college student, I spent Easter break at Daytona Beach (in the late 1960s) talking to hordes of students, many of whom were Catholics. When I asked Catholic students if they believed they would go to heaven at the moment of death, they gave these kinds of answers:

> "Well, I certainly hope so. I can only hope that my good outweighs my bad and that God will take this into consideration, thus finding me worthy of heaven."
>
> "No, I do not think I would go to heaven right now. I am not sure what would happen to me, to tell you the truth."
>
> "I am not sure, but I hope, pray and try. All my life I have sought to be a faithful Catholic and I am still trying to do all that I can."

These are the very answers we would expect if the Catholic mystery is sincerely followed as the way to eternal life. In spite of official denials to the contrary, asserting that the way of salvation is by the grace of God, such answers are far too common with most Catholics. Whatever grace is taught in Catholic doctrine is mixed with the need to *perform* right works in order to be justified.

Here and there, in spite of the dogma of the church, we will hear a different and more biblical answer to the question about entering heaven. In a survey, one Catholic woman said, "I feel as long as you believe in Jesus, and that is all He asks you to do, then you'll be going to heaven." When the interviewer asked this same Catholic woman what she believed about Him she replied, "That He died for you. That He forgives your sins if you believe in Him. And that is all He asks." This answer is much closer to the one we see in the New Testament, yet it is rarely heard from those who are Catholic.

What did Jesus Himself say? "I tell you the truth, whoever hears my word and believes him who sent me has eternal life and will not be condemned; he has crossed over from death to life" (John 5:24). Another New Testament writer wrote, "Faith is being sure of what we hope for and certain of what we do not see" (Hebrews 11:1). Can you see the radical difference such promises will make for the assurance of those who trust Christ only? Those who believe that He is their faithful High Priest can truly rest assured that He has finished the work of redemption. They know that their only obligation is to trust Him alone. He will save, and He will save fully and completely.

I labor, as a teacher of God's holy Word, to avoid unnecessary offense in every way, but this discussion regarding death and purgatory underscores several clear differences between evangelical faith and Catholic faith. The Catholic doctrine, which has no obvious biblical support, causes multitudes to trust the visible church and its sacraments to save them. But in the end this very teaching gives no sure hope of eternal life with our Savior in heaven. I must voice my protest because I love the Word of God and the people of God. This is not a minor difference; it painfully separates evangelical believers from Catholic doctrine and practice. My argument in saying all this to you who are Catholics is not against you as an individual. Rather, it is with your church—a church that I am sure you love, but a church, no less, that has consistently established traditions that are contrary to the Word of God.

PART 3

The Challenge Today

As we move into the twenty-first century, evangelicals are suffering from a kind of historical and doctrinal amnesia. We do not seem to know where we came from or where we are going. We are embracing many agendas without clarity regarding our main agenda—preaching and living the gospel.

Catholics are facing a similar problem in some ways. While for decades masses of Catholics in Europe, South America, and the United States have chosen not to actively practice their faith, now countless numbers are choosing to turn away from the church altogether. In America, for example, Catholic schools, social programs, and charities are in decline. Postmodern thought challenges the solid foundation of a once unquestioned faith.

Having increasingly put aside the old language and harsh rhetoric of the past, evangelicals and Catholics are now discussing unity and what some have called "our common mission." Historic steps have been taken that excite some and confuse many. Further, some well-known evangelicals have converted to Catholicism. How are we to understand these conversions? And how do Catholics respond to the continual loss of their own members to evangelical congregations throughout North America, not to mention Asia, Africa, and Latin America?

For evangelicalism to remain true to both its theological heritage and the Scriptures it professes to follow, we need to learn from the Protestant Reformation the concerns that will help us keep our ship on course. What are these concerns, and are they still important?

CHAPTER TEN

The Present Hour

As time moves onward, some things change, while others seem to remain the same. The Catholic Church has for centuries claimed changelessness. Yet it is quite obvious that a new focus has been emphasized as a result of Vatican II (1962–1965). Most Catholics are pleased by these developments. They allow for a new kind of discussion, and they also allow Catholics and evangelicals to talk to one another without many of the fears of the past. They invite us to listen, to learn, and to grow.

But with these gains there are also some losses. One of the significant losses of the post-Vatican II climate is becoming recognized by more and more conservative Catholics. Rome may not be the same church (in style and form) that existed after the more reactionary deliberations of Trent and Vatican I (1870), but, as a result of embracing the thought of the Enlightenment, the modern Catholic Church increasingly looks more and more like liberal Protestantism. The creed is still officially upheld, but scores of scholars and priests seem to think the creed doesn't matter any more.

Take for instance the work of the *Jesus Seminar*, a group of radical scholars, both Protestant and Catholic, who question the authenticity of the sayings ascribed to Jesus in the New Testament. Their much-publicized work has appeared on the pages of *Time*, *Newsweek,* and other popular news magazines, undermining the biblical record. The question these scholars continually raise is this: "Is the Jesus of history the Jesus revealed in the New Testament?" The end result of the committee's labor is clearly an attempt, deliberate or otherwise, to destroy confidence in the Christ of history, despite the fact that both Catholics and Protestants have consistently confessed faith in the historic Christ.

The rise of modernist theologians in the Catholic Church does not bode well for the future of Catholic theology in the West. Evangelical theologian Robert Strimple sums up the problem:

> The Roman Catholic Church makes a distinction between theology and magisterium, allowing intellectual freedom for theologians but reserving authoritative pronouncements to the magisterium. For the past fifty years the primary characteristic of Roman Catholic theology has been a desire to be truly modern in terms of post-Enlightenment theology. Recent theologians have called into question the meaning of every affirmation of the historic Christian church. Thus, the debate between evangelical Protestant theologians and contemporary Roman Catholic theologians focuses on the most radically fundamental theological issues conceivable.
>
> Many points of comparison exist between modern Catholic theology and liberal Protestant theology. Of special concern is how Roman Catholic theologians have treated the crucial issues of scriptural revelation and inspiration, as well as the relationship between Scripture and tradition. Karl Rahner, the most influential Catholic theologian of our time, embodies this new Roman Catholic theology.[1]

The average lay Catholic is confused by much of this, knowing simply that things have changed and that these changes have not always been improvements. Those who study at Catholic colleges and universities have had to face the implications of this modernist challenge head on. This problem of what has been called the *trahison des clercs* (i.e., the "treason of the intellectuals") has plagued modern Catholicism for over four decades now. In Europe and America it is a particularly vexing problem. Many Catholic professors openly oppose the binding authority of the creeds and catechisms of their own church. They employ critical methods of study that are used to attack the very foundations of the faith. The future of much of the Catholic Church is in danger if theologians continue to follow the secular drift of the culture around them.

Vatican II

Vatican Council II was convened on October 11, 1962, by Pope John XXIII (who died in June 1963). John was the pontiff who desired to "open the windows and let in some fresh air." He charged the council to work in three areas—renewal, modernization, and ecumenism. This general church council did exactly that, finishing its task on December 8, 1965. It was Pope Paul VI who presided over the last three general sessions and served his church during the early years of transition. Sixteen major documents, filling two large volumes, make up the written work of Vatican II.

This council had a revolutionary impact upon both Catholic practice and Catholic self-awareness. It reformed, as we noted earlier, liturgical practice. It also changed the governing styles and ecclesiastical discipline of the church. All of this had an immense impact upon how the average Catholic understands his or her church. No longer would the church be an unchanging bastion of stability and purpose in the modern world.

Some evangelicals argue that nothing fundamental was changed by Vatican II. They argue that since Rome never changes, then nothing substantial has been changed, except for a few minor surface alterations. Most who have studied Vatican II clearly believe otherwise. If evangelicals bother to talk honestly with their Catholic friends they will see that these changes are very real.

Though nothing *central* to the great doctrinal differences has changed since Vatican II, what has changed is how the modern Catholic experiences his own church. For most Catholics this is a welcome change, though movements to restore the past still exist within the church.

George Weigel, a Catholic scholar, writes accurately that Vatican II was a great revolution because of "the transformation of the world's oldest institution from an instrument of the status quo into an instrument of change." Weigel argues that there was a revolution in five areas:[2]

Modernity	The church opened itself up to modern scholarship and thought.
Self-understanding	The church shifted its approach to accommodate lay ministry and calling more eagerly, thus opening the door to greater involvement in liturgy and life by non-ordained men and women.
Liturgy	This includes, but is not limited to, the vernacular Mass.
Relationship to non-Catholics	This is the open door to all other Christians and even to non-Christian groups (ecumenism).
Religious liberty	This is a particularly American contribution to the church, which views the societies of the world as more desirably pluralistic in the sense that it recognizes a more self-conscious separation of religion and state.

Our Sunday Visitor's *Catholic Encyclopedia* sums up the tensions of the post-Vatican II debate in one clear sentence: "Debate over the Council's meaning has been a source of tension, especially where its discontinuity with the preceding Tradition has been exaggerated."[3] This is accurate. It is also a bit of an understatement. These tensions will most likely not go away for some time, especially in the face of the radical new theologies that abound in liberal Catholicism.

Vatican II also opened the door for new discussion with Protestants in general, and more recently with evangelicals in particular. Historic discussions have been held and important documents have been issued. For the first time in more than four centuries there has been meaningful dialogue without fear of reprisal.

But did Vatican II officially change the older doctrines that precipitated the great divide of the sixteenth century? Has Trent been formally *reversed* by these new developments? Not at all. A new formula has been adopted, a new way of thinking has been embraced. But the creeds of the past have plainly been left in place.

Consider this lesson from Protestant history in America: Liberal Protestantism allowed the creeds to remain in place during the past century, while megashifts in belief and practice took place at the same time. Old words were still used, but they were given new and wider meaning. In this approach we still hear of salvation in Christ and of His death and resurrection. But what is meant? The old way meant that a real man died an actual substitutionary atoning death as a sacrifice for sinners. He died under God's curse and was buried. He rose physically on the third day for our justification. The new way speaks of Christ dying, but interprets His death as an *example* for us to follow. As for His physical resurrection, well, it makes no real difference, since He lives in our hearts through our experience of Him! This new way is faulty because it attacks the very historic foundations and doctrinal orthodoxy of the Christian church. As the apostle reasons, "If Christ has not been raised, our preaching is useless and so is your faith" (1 Corinthians 15:14).

The new Catholicism often reinterprets old concepts, dogmas, and life in terms of a new way of thinking. The shift is from old, objective, distinct definitions (as found in Trent and Vatican I) to modern *subjective* experience. The circle is left the same but made much wider. The core is defended, at one level, but the appearance at the outer rim of the circle has changed significantly. For this reason the endless debate among evangelicals about the changes made by Vatican II is often poorly informed. Because many evangelicals do not understand the Catholic doctrine of the incarnate mystery of the visible church, combined with the idea of the evolution of dogma over the centuries, they argue with one another about how much or how little Vatican II really changed things.

It would be far better if evangelicals began to listen to contemporary Catholic apologists and teachers, fully aware of our profound historic differences, but willing, at the same time, to understand one another in our present environment. Vatican II did open a door for this opportunity. The hunger for the knowledge of the Scriptures among countless Catholics is apparent. Should we refuse to teach modern Catholics and poorly taught Protestants the great truths of the Word of God when this is our biblical and evangelical heritage?

Opportunities for the Present Time

Dialogue is one thing. Meaningful agreement is another. Let's not kid ourselves. As we saw in chapters 5–9, major doctrinal differences still remain for Catholics and evangelicals. And the issues that caused the great divide of the sixteenth century are still with us. (We will consider these more directly in chapter 12.) These differences are *not* minor. All of our goodwill cannot make them disappear. Our respective houses, simply put, cannot be united by an appeal to bring them together on the basis of major common denominators.

Opportunities for meaningful cooperation do exist in both of our traditions. Catholics have seen an erosion of confidence in basic moral values among their rank and file in the West. Liberation theology and the rise of radical feminization, gay rights groups, and pro-abortion forces within the Catholic community itself all challenge the historically strong moral position of Roman Catholicism. As Catholics seek for ways to push back these anti-biblical challenges, they often find that evangelicals make positive cobelligerents in these cultural and moral battles.

Evangelicals, increasingly concerned about an eroding moral climate in the public square, find Roman Catholic moral theology well thought out. It is very consistent in its God-centeredness. Catholics often reveal a deeper "fear of God" in terms of personal accountability than that encountered in many modern evangelical communities. They certainly retain a more reverential view of gathered worship, given their view of mystery.

Ronald Nash has written accurately,

> Because evangelical social thought has tended to lag far behind the social and cultural writings of conservative Catholics, a number of conservative Catholic writers have occasionally functioned as mentors to a growing number of conservative evangelical social activists. A short list of such Catholic thinkers would have to include Russell Kirk, William F. Buckley, Jr., Frank Meyer, Michael Novak, Richard John Neuhaus, and George Weigel.[4]

The Tie That Does Not Bind

Because we have experienced increasing unity in areas relating to public policy and cultural concern, and because we have begun to talk to one another more openly, the tendency for some people is to feel that we now have a common mission and purpose. Pope John Paul II, in his bestseller *Crossing the Threshold of Hope*, writes of this very thing:

> Many enthusiastic people, sustained by great optimism, were ready to believe the Second Vatican Council had already resolved the problem. But the Council only opened the road to unity, committing first of all the Catholic Church; but that road itself is a process, which must gradually overcome many obstacles—whether of a doctrinal or a cultural or a social nature—that have accumulated over the course of centuries.[5]

The gains of the present discussion are real. So are the obstacles that remain. To speak of our differences as if they were not real is neither honest nor helpful.

Cobelligerents or Allies?

Over the last three decades evangelical leaders have found themselves working alongside various peoples on numerous projects and concerns. Sometimes this cooperation is political, as in framing concerns regarding foreign policy or international issues. Other times it is more distinctly moral, as in the abortion debate.

How then are evangelicals to relate to Christians from other traditions, to non-Christians, and especially to those who represent traditions plainly contrary to a Christ-centered theology of grace founded in the gospel alone? Evangelicals may find themselves working in local communities with Roman Catholics, Mormons, conservative Jews, and Orthodox Christians. Should we avoid this involvement because we are evangelicals? I think not. Let me give an illustration of how we might think about this type of involvement and our relationship to it.

In the Second World War, England was fighting mightily against Nazi Germany and Hitler. America came into the effort as a strong ally of Great Britain. We had much in common, both politically and socially. Later, the Soviet Union, under Joseph Stalin's leadership, turned against Hitler because of the threat he posed against their nation. At the beginning of the war Hitler and Stalin had been allies. Stalin and Hitler actually shared the common trait of treachery. However, Hitler double-crossed Stalin during the advance of the war, prompting Stalin to turn to England and the United States in his effort to repel Hitler. As nations, we both sided with Stalin because of the mutual threat of Hitler. We were allies in one sense but we were never allies in another more profound sense. Stalin was an ally, but this was an alliance clearly of a different sort than that between Great Britain and the United States, as Churchill and Roosevelt understood. To put it simply, we were, in actuality, *cobelligerents* with Stalin. We could never remain his allies once the war came to an end. We had shared some things in common, but our differences were still quite great.

This is the way relationships work in a fallen world. Two groups may find that they can join together in a common cause that they both understand as beneficial to their mutual interests. But problems will arise when they expect the wrong things from this relationship, such as expecting their cobelligerency to result in a relationship of close allies on *all* matters of doctrinal belief.

Let me illustrate further. Let's say someone invites me to join a group called "Citizens for Life." I gladly join with a number of folks from various religious backgrounds. We are cobelligerents. Another group invites me to join in. It is called "Christians for Life." This is a different matter. Here we now use a word that has different connotations for different people. Evangelicals will generally wish to use the term *Christian* for those who are openly committed to the gospel of Christ and the authority of Scripture. But if they keep joining groups that use such names and terms so broadly, before long the meaning of both the names and terms will diminish. The word *Christian* already means very little in our culture, and the term *evangelical* has lost more and more of its meaning in recent decades. If this continues, the reality behind such words will be drastically reduced as well.

Baptists and Presbyterians have differences regarding some important doctrinal issues, but they also agree on the doctrine of the authority of Scripture and salvation by grace alone. The fact that God is outraged by the murder of unborn infants moves them to be allies in the concern they have regarding abortion. In many cases they can be more than cobelligerents. Why? Because they share a common confessional stance and a common practical view of the grace of God and the Scriptures. They are true evangelical allies in spiritual battles for the gospel of Christ.

Devout Catholics have a high view of life. This is grounded in their moral outrage against murder and their historical theological tradition. Because evangelicals and Catholics have such substantive theological differences, we cannot relate as true allies in the same faith. We can be cobelligerents in important causes, and we can continue to talk to each other in the new spirit of openness. But we cannot, and dare not, overlook the differences that we still have between us. When distinctives are surrendered, both sides run the risk of losing truths vital to their own identity.

For evangelicals the twentieth-century rise of modern evangelistic methodology has often united Catholics and evangelicals in common causes to reach people and to appeal for a personal decision for Christ. This commonly accepted goal in evangelism very often follows the path of doctrinal fuzziness, if for no other reason than to get as many people as possible to "make a decision for Christ." Evangelicals, in particular, need to pray for much greater clarity in this whole matter. If they do not they will soon lose far more than they gain. The doctrine of conversion is simply not a big enough foundation upon which to build a whole movement. For that matter, the "new birth" is not a big enough foundation either. There is much more to solid evangelical faith than these commonly preached truths.

At this point, some people will ask, "Really, how important are these doctrinal differences? Can't Catholics and evangelicals be more than cobelligerents and become real allies in the present secular society?" No. Our differences are still so important that Rome continues to believe that it alone is truly the church of Christ. Pope John Paul II writes,

> Christ is the true active subject of humanity's salvation. The Church is as well, inasmuch as it acts on behalf of Christ and in Christ. Christ . . . asserted the need for the Church, when men enter through baptism as if through a door. For this reason men cannot be saved who do not want to enter or remain in the Church, knowing that the Catholic Church was founded by God through Christ as a necessity.[6]

Roman Catholic documents do speak openly of ecumenism and unity. Evangelicals need to understand that this plea is essentially quite plain—we evangelicals may be "separated brethren" who can be saved outside the visible means of the true Catholic Church, but truth would best be served if ultimately we came back to the Mother Church. It is both the design of the writers of many of these documents and the prayer of the present Catholic spiritual leadership that we (as evangelicals) return to the conciliar, creedal, Petrine Roman Church.

This last point cannot be overstated in our present context. What Vatican II clearly taught about ecumenism is: 1) Catholics need to be made continually aware that the church Christ established was the Roman Church with its bishops and the pope as its head. This church alone was given the mystery of the Holy Eucharist. 2) Non-Catholic Christians, who are justified by their baptism, are to be viewed as "separated brethren." They have a valid means of salvation but are not yet part of the church in its fullness. 3) All Catholics should promote ecumenism by not making unfair criticism of other Christians. And to promote this third point the Vatican officially recognizes appointed experts in theology who are commissioned to dialogue with various other Christians and groups. But make no mistake about the goal of Vatican II in all of this. The "Decree of Ecumenism" states plainly:

> The results will be that, little by little, as the obstacles to perfect ecclesiastical communion are overcome, all Christians will be gathered, in a common celebration of the Eucharist, into the unity of the one and only Church, which Christ bestowed on his Church from the beginning. Thus unity, we believe, subsists in the Catholic Church as something she can never lose, and we hope that it will continue to increase until the end of time (Second Vatican Council, "Decree on Ecumenism," no. 4).

And the 1994 catechism adds: "Concern for achieving unity 'involves the whole Church, faithful and clergy alike.' But we must realize 'that this holy objective—of all Christians in the unity of the one and only Church of Christ—transcends human powers and gifts.'"[7]

Any discussions of unity must, if they are not naively considered, understand that Rome's clearly *confessed* understanding is that evangelicals are, necessarily, *outside* the true church. Ultimately, the goal of all such efforts is to bring all who confess faith in Christ "home to Rome."

Summing Up

Historically, evangelicals have believed that there are three visible marks that determine a faithful New Testament church: a proper preaching of the gospel; a proper doctrine of the sacraments; and a proper biblical discipline. Evangelicals cannot, by their own confession and faith, believe that Roman Catholicism is a standing, faithful New Testament church. The Catholic Church certainly does not believe local evangelical churches are true, faithful, confessing New Testament congregations. Such churches are without the magisterium, without the central mystery of the Mass, and without the practice of the other six sacraments. According to Catholic faith, how can they possibly be "true" churches?

We must not personally judge the ultimate standing before God of any *individual* soul. As Scripture says, "The Lord knows those who are his" (2 Timothy 2:19), and, "To his own master he [each person] stands or falls" (Romans 14:4). What we must insist upon, however, is that the New Testament is neither vague nor ambiguous when it reveals what a church is (in its essence) and what its message and practices are to be. Evangelicals, by definition, believe that Rome neither confesses nor teaches the apostolic gospel. Evangelicals, furthermore, believe that Rome does not administer and teach the sacraments properly. Because of these theological beliefs, sad to say, evangelicals are obligated to conclude with the Reformers that "Rome is a fallen church!"

Because we believe Rome is fallen, we must urge Roman Catholics, and all others who profess allegiance to Jesus Christ within any tradition, to trust Christ alone for salvation. As faithful evangelicals we must continue to clearly preach justification by faith alone, through grace alone. This means that individual Catholics must trust in Him, not in the Catholic mystery with its system of sacraments and personal devotion, but in and through the message of the gospel. Most evangelicals would agree with me in saying that some Catholics really are trusting Christ savingly, but this saving faith is formally in spite of the actual teaching of their church, not *because* of it.

After years of intense struggling with Scriptures, a friend came to believe that Rome was a fallen church and made the difficult choice of leaving his birth community. He writes poignantly:

> The current discussions about the unity and nature of the church touch home with me in a very real way. The question I wrestled with for several long years was this: "Did I really leave the Holy Catholic Church?" This question is a daunting one for any earnest Catholic. This may be the question either you or someone you know is pondering. My search for peace ended, ultimately, by finding the answer to a similar question: "Is the Roman Catholic Church truly a fallen church?" The answer, I found, lies in what constitutes a fallen church. Seeing as how the chief treasure of the true church is in the gospel of Jesus Christ, and how the chief mandate given to that church is the Great Commission, then the entire matter, for me, was finally resolved when I had studied Rome's gospel message.
>
> I concluded, after painful struggle, that if the Catholic system of baptismal regeneration, progressive justification, the dispensation of grace through her priesthood via the sacraments, human merit co-mingled with Christ's redemptive work, purgatorial suffering for the expiation of "venial" sins, the propitiatory nature of the Mass, the intercession of Mary and the saints, and the uncertainty of one's eternal destiny, is the way of salvation espoused by the Catholic Church—and it is—then this elaborate synergistic and sacerdotal system would have to be judged before the bar of Holy Scripture. And this is exactly what I set out to do. From 1991 until 1996, I wrestled with whether or not the church of my childhood, the church which I loved since a young boy, did indeed propagate a false gospel message. If it did, then no matter how orthodox its doctrine of the Trinity or how high its Christology or how beautiful its liturgy, I would be compelled to state what I approached ever so cautiously: the Church of Rome is a fallen church.

How, then, should we handle our serious differences? Especially when both sides take so seriously the nature of the church? I answer: with respect and true Christian love. We are obligated to love God fully and our neighbors as ourselves. Surely there is plenty here for us to work on if we really look at our differences without glossing over them. And surely the Scripture enjoins true charity upon all who sincerely name the name of the Lord.

CHAPTER ELEVEN

Is Evangelical Really Enough?

In the name of common cause and concern there have recently been concerted efforts to express Roman Catholic and evangelical unity. One well-known example is the much-heralded document "Evangelicals and Catholics Together: The Christian Mission in the Third Millennium" (ECT, 1994). This declaration has been hailed as a great step toward unity between Catholics and evangelicals. If the statement had simply been an expression of political and social cobelligerency, much of the furor that was caused would have died down long ago. The problem is this: theological language is plainly used throughout this document, and the gospel is *not* clearly affirmed in the areas where it should have been if biblical unity in mission were the actual purpose. Sadly, many evangelical church members are confused, and a debate continues to rage, often with little understanding of what may really be at stake.

"Evangelicals and Catholics Together"

The accord itself was a 25-page document prepared by some 15 leading evangelical and Roman Catholic spokesmen and signed by another 25 or so leading evangelicals and Roman Catholics. It is neither official nor ecclesiastically sanctioned by any representative church body. It serves as an informal treatment of issues that are believed to be points for unity in an honest expression of cobelligerence against an increasingly hostile culture. Full-length books, articles, editorials, and other verbal presentations have been done in earnest—all seeking to explain the document and the course outlined by it. Why the fuss if we do really have so much in common?

To begin with, the language of the document is theologically soft. It begins with a quotation from John Paul II that this is "a springtime of world missions." It then adds, "As Christ is one, so the Christian mission is one." The implication seems clear—Catholics and evangelicals have "one [common] mission."

But do we really have substantial agreement between Rome and biblical evangelicalism on the mission of the church? Not if we take seriously the present theology confessed and practiced by the Catholic Church. Evangelicals may be "separated brethren" according to Vatican II, but the intention of the Catholic Church has been, and remains, to bring evangelicals into communion with the pope and the ministry of the "true" church (cf. chapter 10). For evangelicals, *the mission of the church is to preach the gospel and carry out the great commission* (see Matthew 28:18-20). If we are faithful to our confessional understanding of the gospel, we will do this only when men and women are brought to Christ alone, by grace alone, through faith alone.

Evangelicals confess that the universal church—that is, the body of Christ—is made up of His elect. Such may be found in many places. Some Christians may even be in places where the gospel is not faithfully preached. Some believe the gospel in spite of the doctrinal errors of a particular church, be it Roman Catholic or Protestant.

Because evangelicals love the church and believe John 17 (Christ's prayer for unity), they too must labor for the unity of the visible church. But we also understand that compromising the gospel is a grave sin. It is a cancer that will destroy the life of true faith. To talk about common cause and then refer to it as a "common mission" with those whose church confessionally denies the gospel of grace is to seriously distort our mission.

Without the gospel there cannot be a standing church. (We remember that Luther correctly said that justification by faith alone is *the* article of a standing or falling church.) Rome does not confess the gospel. As we have seen repeatedly, she denies grace alone and faith alone by her constant mixture of grace and works. Some individual Catholics do savingly trust Christ and believe the essential elements of the gospel, but this does not unite us, as representatives of our respective communions, in "common mission." If evangelicals are to remain diligent for the gospel, I am afraid that documents like ECT will properly trouble evangelicals who are committed to the essential elements of their Reformation and evangelical heritage.

The document turns, in a second section, to areas of agreement. This is titled "We Affirm Together." Here we find listed the areas of agreement in the arena of cobelligerency. The problem is that the document states, "We affirm together that we *are justified by grace through faith* because of Christ" (emphasis added). At first glance that sounds very promising, but do you notice what is *missing* here? The essential qualifier made famous by the Reformers—the word *only*, or *alone*. The evangelical cannot notice this omission without serious concern.

The document goes on to plea for greater visible unity and less polemical debate. Then the areas of remaining disagreement between evangelicals and Catholics are mentioned. Here again there is a serious problem. Several points of difference are listed, including:

- "The church as an integral part of the Gospel or the church as a communal consequence of the Gospel."
- "The church as a visible communion or invisible fellowship of true believers."
- "The sole authority of Scripture (*sola scriptura*) or Scripture as authoritatively interpreted in the church."
- "Ministry ordered in apostolic succession or the priesthood of all believers."
- "Remembrance of Mary and the saints or devotion to Mary and the saints."
- "Baptism as a sacrament of regeneration or testimony to regeneration."

But, astonishing as it may be, the material principle of the Reformation is not mentioned anywhere in this list—justification by grace *alone* through faith *alone*. In Section I of this document we read that the signers "Affirm Together" that "Jesus is Lord.... And [that] there is salvation in no one else (Acts 4)." Further, we read (in Section I), "We affirm together that we are justified by grace through faith because of Christ." Thus, the most important doctrinal formulation of the evangelical cause, namely justification by faith alone, is sadly missing from this much-discussed affirmation. As we have shown throughout this book, this essential doctrine still divides us, yet this much-praised document left it out. But that is not all. Some of our significant disagreements are not correctly stated, as you will note in the above list. But the ultimate result is an unhelpful misconstruction of the *real* meaning of very important theological issues.

Finally, the document ends with two sections titled "We Contend Together" and "We Witness Together." Here evangelicals have further cause for concern when they read that Protestants and Catholics should not "proselytize" one another. This is regarded by the document as "sheep stealing." Some who signed the declaration have defended this statement by saying that it was not meant to say we should not evangelize members of other churches but simply that we should not overtly, consciously, seek to lead people out of the church they are presently communing with. I am afraid that this is a distinction with a meaningless difference.

If Catholics believe they are in fellowship with the true church, in union with Christ through apostolic succession and Petrine leadership, then they must, by their own definition, desire for me as an evangelical to come into union with the true church. They would desire this because they believe their understanding is correct and because it would be in my own best interest to commune with them in the true church. If I, as an evangelical, believe that Rome is a fallen church and in serious need of both proper biblical authority (Scripture alone) and a proper gospel (grace alone and faith alone), then I must love Catholics enough to urge them to seek a church that provides gospel fellowship. I must urge them to make their conscience captive to the Word of God, not to me as a teacher, or to the pope or any other human authority.

I maintain, with my evangelical forefathers who carefully searched the Scriptures, that Christ intends for Christians to have unity, but it must be *a unity in the truth*. Personal Christian unity cannot be established with anyone who preaches a gospel other than the one delivered by our Lord and His apostles (see Galatians 1:6-9). True ecclesiastical unity, between church communions, certainly cannot be established with a church that does not affirm the gospel of God's grace. Any version of the gospel that falls short of the evangel of the New Testament is inadequate and ultimately hurtful.

Surely both evangelicals and Catholics can strive to be people of goodwill. At the same time we can understand that the gulf which still divides us is not primarily political or sociological. It is, and always has been, *theological*. The issues that we have considered in this book are not matters of style, dress, form, or ritual. They are matters of biblical and theological substance. To take a minimalist approach that glosses over serious differences will never lead to biblical reformation or promote spiritual revival.

Some of the evangelicals who signed ECT are aware of the great doctrinal differences that remain between us. Why, then, would they sign this document? My short answer, having discussed this with several signers and having read a number of written explanations and defenses, is expressed in the paragraphs that follow.

Some evangelical signers of ECT believe that they are developing, through this kind of process, an "ecumenism of the trenches." They argue that since evangelicals and Catholics have many common doctrinal convictions—Creation, the Fall, substitutionary atonement, the infallibility of the Scriptures—they need to experience a deeper unity practically. Others cite the Apostles' Creed as the basis for common ground. They want to be sure that Christians really are fighting against the true enemies of our faith, not against those who are fighting alongside us in the trenches of this modern war in the defense of the truth.[1]

The idea of a "Great Tradition Christianity," which can be found in confessional and orthodox Christianity historically, is also cited as a basis for a certain kind of unity. Again, here is an idea that is quite helpful, so long as we recognize the necessity for uniting believers in a common mission as articulated by the gospel. There is a great Christian tradition and evangelicals not only need to understand this tradition much better, they also need to embrace more wholly some of the significant contributions of this great tradition.

Does this mean that the two great theological principles that have stood in stark contrast to Catholic dogma for nearly five centuries have been reconciled? Can evangelicals now form an alliance with those who hold to a confessional stance that opposes the gospel and the authority of the Scriptures? Until evangelicals once again understand the gospel properly, they will remain in grave danger when they engage in discussions regarding relationships with other communions.

"The Gift of Salvation"

In late 1997 a second document was published by the magazine *First Things*, following the pattern of the earlier statement just surveyed. This statement went a long way towards clearing up some of the problems raised by ECT. *Christianity Today*, the flagship periodical of evangelicalism in North America, referred to this second statement as "a remarkable statement on what we mean by the gospel."

This new statement was more forthrightly doctrinal than the first one. It addressed the central problem raised by the first initiative—namely, in what sense do we share a common doctrine of salvation? "The Gift of Salvation" openly concludes that justification is by faith alone (*sola fide*), as well as by grace alone (*sola gratia*). This statement, signed by several very prominent Catholic spokespersons, was also signed by several excellent evangelical thinkers who clearly articulate the gospel message as it is outlined in this book.

This new statement genuinely aims at dealing with the central issues of the gospel message. It fails, however, as such short statements often do, to deal with several matters that have consistently underscored the real theological differences between Catholics and evangelicals. I have in mind here the doctrine of imputation. *Sola fide* is not merely a slogan to be rallied around by modern Christians. The central issue, doctrinally, in the sixteenth century, at least when it came to discussing the gospel itself, was disagreement over the meaning of imputation. Are sinners put right with God *solely* on the basis of an *alien righteousness* that is *extra nos* (i.e., outside of themselves), or is there anything they do in believing and responding that causes the grace of God to come to them on the basis of something *within* them? Because modern evangelicals have so frequently stressed the new birth, and accepting Christ into the heart by faith, they have essentially lost their grip on this central idea of the Reformation message—i.e., God declares us right on the basis of what is done by Christ outside of our hearts before He does anything to sanctify us inwardly. Our standing before God is based entirely on what Christ did, not what we do, even in our believing the gospel.

This second statement of faith has fostered some new discussion among evangelicals about the very meaning of the gospel itself. Such discussions may actually help evangelical Christians better understand that their real spiritual unity and strength lie in getting the gospel right, not in standing together around various issues. It can be hoped that this ongoing process might actually lead to greater clarification, among evangelicals, of the gospel itself. It is difficult to talk about unity in the gospel when there is little agreement regarding the essential nature of the gospel message.

With an increased interest in biblical and textual studies growing within the modern Catholic Church, evangelicals (especially serious scholars from our ranks) should be prepared to increase their efforts to discuss important conclusions with Catholics. Some of these scholars, and others who have followed their efforts to get at the vital message of the New Testament by means of careful exegesis, do actually believe the gospel. This conclusion, however, does not change the fact that the Roman Catholic Church, in its present confessional position, is not a faithful Christian communion.

Some common ground has been found between *some* Catholics and *some* evangelicals. Common ideological foes have been more clearly identified. And common core beliefs, as seen in "Great Tradition Christianity," are being more freely discussed by evangelicals and Catholics as we come to the end of this millennium. There are some hopeful signs in all of this, but there are also some dangerous rapids to be navigated. Only evangelicals who understand and affirm the gospel are truly capable of profitably entering into such dialogue with a positive outcome.

But Don't We Already Have True Consensus?

As we have shown several times already, faithful practicing Catholics believe, according to their church's confessional position, that the Roman Catholic Church is the one true church. They believe it has an infallible authority in its magisterium, as taught by Jesus Christ. They believe that God has preserved their church inviolate in apostolic tradition from the first century all the way to the present.

But as former Catholic William Webster notes, "The claims for Roman Catholic authority cannot be supported by the facts of history or the truth of Scripture. In reality the Roman Catholic Church has departed from the teaching of the historic Catholic Church and can no longer be rightly described as catholic, but as Roman."[2] The supposed consensus of the early church fathers is a myth often set forward and hardly ever seriously questioned. However, one Catholic Patrologist scholar (i.e., a student of early church writers), Boniface Ramsey, concludes:

> Sometimes, then, the fathers speak and write in a way that would eventually be seen as unorthodox. But this is not the only difficulty with respect to the criterion of orthodoxy. The other great one is that we look in vain in many of the fathers for references to things that many Christians might believe in today. We do not find, for instance, some teachings on Mary or the papacy that were developed in medieval and modern times.[3]

Rome does affirm many truths that are both catholic and apostolic. We began this book by quoting the Apostles' Creed, a commonly held statement that unites us in some important truths. The problem is with what Rome has *added*—i.e., with what evolved in both Rome's faith and practice over the centuries. The evangelical, on the other hand, believes that the problem is not with doctrines added by the Reformers but with the doctrines that needed to be recovered. We dare not add to the teachings of the New Testament. This is, for serious confessional evangelicals, the bottom line (see Revelation 22:18-19).

Roman Catholic apologists justify their church's tradition on the basis of their theory of doctrinal development. By this they mean that certain doctrines were *implicit* in the early church, but became explicit as the magisterium defined and explained them over time. Evangelicals reject this claim outright. The principle of *unanimous consent*, by which it is argued that there is agreement among the early fathers in a particular area of teaching, will not hold up at many points where Catholic apologists seek to defend these added doctrines and practices. William Webster has ably demonstrated that "what we discover is not a *development* of truth but a *departure* from it. Roman Catholic teaching in its exaltation of tradition, the papacy, and the church is a depreciation of the authority of Scripture and the supreme authority of Jesus Christ."[4]

The supposed consensus that evangelicals and Catholics have does exist if we limit the ground of our agreement to basic moral issues. And it certainly exists in truths such as the doctrine of Christ and the Trinity (see chapter 1)—truths that are part of the "Great Tradition" as we have called it. At the same time the great truths rediscovered by evangelical Reformers in the sixteenth century are often unimportant to many who now call themselves evangelicals. One reason appears to be this: Many evangelicals no longer clearly understand what it means to be an evangelical. Another reason may be modern evangelicals' unwritten policy of working alongside virtually everyone who has evangelistic zeal. In our desire to get people into the kingdom we often fail to grasp the simple fact that the message of the gospel itself is the power of God unto salvation.

If we do not clearly confess, understand, and defend our message properly we will eventually lose our true power. We may continue to engage in political and social agendas, even adding that we affirm the gospel, while at the same time running a serious risk of losing our unity as evangelicals, which is found only in the message of the gospel itself.

Is "Evangelical" Really Enough?

A number of noted evangelicals have converted to Catholicism in recent days. When this happens a considerable interest is aroused among thinking Christians. Kim Riddlebarger, in an excellent analysis of this movement of evangelicals toward Rome, suggests two primary reasons.

First, there are those like Thomas Howard, formerly an English professor at Gordon College (Massachusetts). Howard, particularly well known through his own writings and because he is Elisabeth Elliot's brother, left evangelicalism because he felt "incomplete." A lack of stress upon history, liturgy, the sacraments, and aesthetics all attracted him to leave evangelicalism.

Howard first became interested in liturgy while a student at Wheaton College (Illinois). He refers to attending an Episcopal church and "feeling guilty about it." Catholic authors increasingly became his "tutors" over several decades, and finally he came to the conclusion that the Catholic Church was "the appointed guardian of the Scriptures." Howard, in an interview with *Christianity Today*, argued that the unity between Christ and His church leads to the question of authority, and that lead him to the magisterium. He adds, "Also important for me was the sacramental understanding of the nature of reality, the nature of God, the world, revelation, the gospel, and the Incarnation."[5]

Thomas Howard not only left a visible, local, evangelical church communion, but he also embraced traditional Catholic doctrine. He replied to a question by Professor John Woodbridge by saying, "I would espouse the traditional Catholic view set forth at the Council of Trent, which loudly asserts justification by faith."[6]

Like so many evangelicals who think they have so much in common with Rome regarding salvation, Howard does not demonstrate a *clear* grasp of the real issues debated by the Council of Trent. As we have already seen, Trent pronounced an anathema upon evangelical believers *not* for teaching justification by faith but for teaching justification by *faith alone*. The word *alone* was the key word upon which the whole debate hinged. A host of other issues flow from this one little word, as we shall see (chapter 12).

It was Howard who wrote, while still an evangelical, a small book with an interesting title: *Evangelical Is Not Enough*.[7] I still remember when I first read this book in 1984, shortly after it was published. I marked in the frontispiece of my copy, "If this is what evangelicalism really is then I believe the author will convert to Catholicism if he is consistent!" Why did I say this?

Howard's book is a powerful apologetic against an American type of evangelicalism that has been popular since World War I. In this kind of evangelicalism, creeds, community, and history are *virtually* unknown. Certain doctrines have been made central to the faith, but whole areas of vital biblical truth are left out. Worship in this kind of evangelicalism is quite often man-centered (entertainment-oriented?), while preaching is often non-doctrinal and even anti-intellectual. I have seen a number of my friends leave this kind of Christianity, thinking that this is the only kind of evangelical faith and practice that exists. Sadly, I can understand why certain people like Howard convert to Rome, but I am still convinced they have abandoned the gospel.

There is a second category of convert who leaves evangelicalism. This type can be seen in the former conservative Presbyterian minister Scott Hahn (see chapter 5). Hahn's conversion (along with that of his wife, Kimberly, the daughter of a famous Presbyterian minister) is well chronicled in their readable autobiography *Rome Sweet Home: Our Journey to Catholicism*.[8] Hahn, who now teaches at Franciscan University of Steubenville

(Ohio) and is a popular apologist for the Catholic Church, converted because he embraced the very Catholic dogmas upon which the Reformation was initially debated.

His interests are more plainly theological than Howard's. Hahn is a skilled debater and a well-educated and conscientious student. For Hahn the two great theological dominoes that fell were (in order) "faith alone" and "Scripture alone." (We will consider these even more carefully in the final chapter.) What makes Hahn so different from other recent converts to Catholicism is this: He pushes his offensive against evangelicalism at precisely the critical points. He understands that the Protestant Reformation was advanced because of two primary theological issues.

What can we say about these well-known converts? First, it would help if we sought to better understand *why* some of these articulate people left evangelicalism. Second, contemporary evangelicalism is in a state of general theological disarray. This leaves it open to such conversions. The answer to this is to recover an evangelicalism that is virile, thoughtful, doctrinal, and God-centered. Finally, we need a better understanding of our Protestant heritage as evangelicals, or we will continue to make the kinds of mistakes that encourage people to leave us.

We must remember that this crossing of the bridge to Rome has a reverse flow of traffic as well. Multitudes of people are going in the opposite direction converting to evangelical faith and leaving Rome for a church centered upon the gospel. On this side of the street the names of prominent people can also be cited, but they may not be as well known as Thomas Howard or Scott Hahn. One of the very reasons Scott Hahn labors as he does with *Catholic Answers* (a Catholic lay apologetics ministry based in San Diego, California) is that he is trying to stop the large flow of Catholic converts to evangelicalism.

Those of us who labor in preaching the gospel have generally seen more conversions to faith in Christ among Catholics than any other group of people, both in North America and overseas.

This is especially true in Latin America, where the rate of conversions to evangelical faith greatly alarms Catholic leaders as we enter the new millennium. Some of the fastest-growing evangelical churches in the world are located in nations where the most traditional Catholicism has long been the religion of the multitudes. As long as the gospel is clearly understood, loved, and preached with compassion, I do not expect this flow to decrease. Both evangelicals and Catholics must discuss this phenomenal growth, via professions of faith in Christ, and find new ways to decrease the hostility that it sometimes produces.

How should evangelicals respond to these publicized conversions, as well as to the major efforts recently under way to unite our evangelical cause with Catholics in a *common mission*?

Summing Up: A Better Way

It is important that we understand what is going on all around us today. The issues faced by the modern church are a grave threat in many ways. Catholics and evangelicals do have significant common ground upon which to face certain enemies.

Furthermore, it is important for evangelicals to recognize that what is *essential* to the message of the gospel itself is not necessarily what is *essential* for individuals to fully understand in order to be saved. Let me explain, as this is a very important and carefully nuanced point. It is *absolutely* essential for salvation that you trust Christ, and only Christ, to save you. If you are trusting in your own "good works" to add to or to complete your believing (for example, Christ does 99 percent and I do only 1 percent) then it is seriously in doubt if you are *truly* trusting Christ as your Savior. The danger for many Catholics here is clear. The Catholic mystery teaches you that there is something quite different than trust in Christ alone as the basis for your justification before God.

In my mind there can be no doubt that there are people who truly believe in Christ who cannot explain forensic justification (or the doctrine of imputation). Indeed, evangelical churches are filled with such people. Serious evangelicals need to remember that you are not saved by *knowing doctrinal truths* and refuting doctrinal errors. You are saved by Christ or you are not saved at all. And the ground upon which Christ saves is the ground of trust alone, or real faith.

But does this mean that imputation, or forensic righteousness, is unimportant? Not at all. To deny this great evangelical truth is to deny Christ and the grace by which He saves us. If meritorious works are a necessary condition for salvation, as Rome has consistently taught since the Council of Trent, then ultimately Catholicism actually denies the grace of God. She may affirm that grace is necessary, as she does throughout the *Catechism of the Catholic Church* (1994), but she denies that it is grace alone that ultimately saves. This means, quite plainly, that she has a gospel that is *not* the gospel of the New Testament.

Because this observation is true I would suggest that the better way to proceed is for evangelicals to maximize their own grip on the gospel in the coming years. We need a much better understanding of the great, historic truths of faith alone, grace alone, and Christ alone. We need to study the Scriptures with more openness and with a deep desire to be radically changed by them. And we need to seek a deeper understanding of the important debates that have shaped and formed our historic churches. We dare not build our theology in a vacuum, as if we can study the Scriptures privately, without the input of faithful men and women who have loved Christ and the gospel in centuries past. Here a proper consensus of truth must be sought and found.

The Holy Spirit will make plain to the people of God the truths of Christ's gospel if they search the Word in dependence upon the Spirit. This too is part and parcel of the evangelical way. This too has preceded the great recoveries of the past. May another such recovery take place in our time!

CHAPTER TWELVE

Recovering Biblical Christianity

My assumption all through this book has been that evangelical faith in Christ is in accord with the teaching of the Scriptures. It is, in a word, orthodox. In this final chapter I will try to show why true, biblical, historic evangelical Christianity is faithful to the principles of Scripture and, as a result, why evangelicals must still stand outside the Church of Rome.

If we are to remain faithful to the Scriptures and to the Lord Jesus Christ, we must "contend earnestly for the faith which was once for all delivered to the saints" (Jude 3 NASB). If we will not stand where the church has courageously stood before and if we will not properly defend the faith, we will ultimately give away our greatest treasure—the authority of the Word of God. I am not suggesting that we do this intentionally. But if we do not speak with the clearest voice where the faith is under attack, we will run from the battle and ultimately lose the heritage given to us by faithful teachers.

If we lose our grip on Scripture, we will also lose our grip on the gospel. This message is our power. It defines us as those who affirm the evangel. This means that we believe people are made right with God through Christ alone, by grace alone, through faith alone. If we fail to understand and teach these Reformation truths, we stand to lose more than any of us can imagine.

These great principles were at the center of the debate in the sixteenth century. They must still be at the center of consistent evangelical faith and practice. They must be recovered once again and not simply by scholars. An army of ordinary believers needs to search the Scriptures afresh and understand that these are grand biblical truths that are worth defending and worth teaching to our children. The present-day disunity and confusion reveals our great loss. We have drifted far away from the truth. And as a result, we are charting uncertain and difficult waters.

Four Distinguished *Solas*

As we saw in chapter 3, the Protestant Reformation of nearly 500 years ago was fundamentally about theology. It was not simply a movement to purge the church of abusive practices, such as the sale of indulgences. Nor was it about claims to spiritual power associated with relics and visits to shrines. In this chapter we want to understand what the primary theological concerns of the Reformers were and why they insisted that these concerns clearly framed their theological position.

Because Latin was still the language of the academy in the sixteenth century, the arguments of the Reformers were often framed in that language. That is why you still hear slogans with names such as *sola gratia* and *sola fide*. What exactly were these four *solas*, and what does each mean?

1. *Sola gratia.* This expression refers to grace alone, or, literally, solely by grace. Simply put, God's saving activity is outside of the human sinner. It is focused in the person of Jesus Christ, and the *sole* ground of His saving work is grace. Grace plus nothing saves the sinner. The grace that saves is given

solely because of God's initiative, since nothing in people prompts God to save undeserving rebels.

2. *Solus Christus.* Christ's doing and dying on our behalf is the *sole* basis of our acceptance and continued fellowship with God. Even our fellowship with God must be Christ-centered. The Holy Spirit's ministry is primarily to glorify Christ and to make Him known. Christ is the *beginning* and *end* of Christian faith and Christian experience.

3. *Sola fide.* The Holy Spirit's gift of faith and repentance to the sinner comes through the hearing of a historical, objective gospel message and is received through faith alone. This means that Christ's substitutionary life and death is imputed to us for justification unto eternal life. The justified sinner receives the Holy Spirit through faith in the gospel, and the one justified will glory only in Christ's cross, making God's saving action in Christ the central affirmation of Christian witness. He will be careful to obey God and please Him in all things revealed in Scripture through continual repentance. But his glory will never be in the feeble efforts of his own life or in the Spirit's presence within him. The Spirit within will lead him to look outward to Christ in every way.

4. *Sola Scriptura.* The Bible and the Bible alone is the Christian's infallible rule (canon) for all faith and practice. It alone is sufficient to establish the believer in the truth, and it alone will determine what he must believe as truth and what he must reject. It is sufficient to accomplish the work of the Spirit in leading us into all righteousness. Its central message, namely, salvation in Christ, is plain for all to see when it is approached in faith. No creeds, councils, or human leaders can act properly in matters of faith and practice except by doing so under the final authority of the written Scriptures.

These, in simple form, are the four great theological pillars of the Reformation. Much more can and should be said, but for now you need to understand that it is for these great truths that evangelicals contend today when they insist on simple loyalty to the Word of God.

GRACE ALONE

Martin Luther did not rediscover the theology of grace. What he rediscovered were the Pauline texts regarding its true meaning. And theologians since Luther have not manufactured a "straw man" for the purpose of an ongoing debate. A proper understanding of grace is ultimately at the heart of every theological error regarding the nature of salvation. Either we have a religion that saves solely on the basis of God's grace, or we have a religion in which we somehow share in saving ourselves. The popular version of self-help religion in America can be heard in the oft-quoted statement (of Benjamin Franklin) that "God helps those who help themselves!" Our part may seem quite small to us. It may even be our decision or our human will that made the real difference. In the end, any system of doctrine that attributes anything to human beings regarding salvation challenges the sovereignty of God's free grace.

Medieval theologians wrote and spoke frequently of grace. What it meant for them was this: Grace was something that God put within a human being so that he could cooperate with God, receiving the divine help that was needed to be justified before a holy God. Even Augustine, the greatest theologian of grace in the early church, was slightly off on this crucial point, thinking of grace as something God deposited within the human soul.

As a good and conscientious Augustinian monk, Luther longed to be acceptable and pleasing to God. His problem was not simply an overworked conscience. He fervently believed that God was radically holy. He believed that God's law was perfect. He believed he had been given grace in his baptism and that he was continually given grace in the sacraments. He even believed that he needed to trust Christ as his Savior. His problem was simple—being a good medieval theologian, he believed that if he could apprehend enough of the inward grace of the Spirit in his own soul he might eventually become righteous before God. But the more he looked inward, the more he saw darkness and sin. He was devastated. All he could hope for was God's judgment, which should justly cast him into perdition.

Modern readers often find Luther's vexed soul disturbing. The reason for this is that our own view of sin is too slight. We are not truly aware of how far we have fallen from the law of God. We are prone to think that God owes us something because we are not really that bad. If God will give us a bit of help we can cooperate, and all will then be well. Luther knew better because he knew the human heart by the revelation of the Spirit to his own heart.

On reading Paul's letter to the Romans Luther discovered that it was only grace that made a sinner right with God. This grace was totally different from an inward endowment. Paul declared that sinners are "justified freely by his grace" (3:24) and added, "For we maintain that a man is justified by faith apart from observing the law" (verse 28). Later, he said, "To the man who does not work but trusts God who justifies the wicked, his faith is credited as righteousness" (4:5).

Where Paul says in Romans 3:24 that we are "justified freely by his grace," some versions correctly say, "justified as a gift." The word for "gift" here means, simply, "without cause." God accepts the sinner quite apart from anything within him. Justifying grace is God's attitude of mercy and favor to lost, undeserving, rebellious sinners. Grace is not to be found in the heart of a person. It is in God's heart alone! Even when true believers reflect grace in their actions, they do so only as a result of this grace that is in God's heart. This is the perspective of grace alone.

If any one insight distinguishes Luther as the father of the Reformation movement, it is this. Reformers who preceded Luther, such as Wycliff and Hus, saw many truths clearly but still lacked this Pauline perspective: *Grace means being totally accepted by God in spite of being totally unacceptable in one's self!*

But doesn't this mean that we can sin with boldness, or without consequence? That is the question Luther's opponents posed when he stated this great truth. But we don't need to turn to Luther to find an answer since Paul's critics responded to him in the same manner when he stated this same truth to the Romans. After presenting the doctrine of grace for several chapters, Paul wrote, "What shall we say, then? Shall we go on sinning so that grace may increase?" (Romans 6:1). His answer is a simple Greek construction, in Romans 6:2, that literally says, "*God forbid!*"

When we understand grace properly, it will raise the identical question for us. If this question never occurs to us, then we have not yet understood or preached grace biblically. It is just that simple.

And when we understand grace in this proper way we will no longer see it as merely necessary. It will be seen as the singular sufficient cause of salvation, without which we would have no hope whatsoever. We will understand that we were born into this world spiritually dead and therefore are completely unable to cooperate with the work of God's grace (even by the Holy Spirit) unless, and until, God is pleased to give us true life (see John 3:3-5; Ephesians 1:11; 2:8-9; Titus 3:3-7).

Christ Alone

The Reformers were quite concerned that grace, improperly understood, could be used as an excuse for sin. The idea that grace springs from a kind of easygoing grandfatherly God who overlooks shortcomings and failures with sweet benevolence was unknown to the theologians of the Reformation. To Luther, for example, God was a sin-hating majestic being who was terrible in His holiness. He was able to cast both body and soul into hell. Grace, therefore, was not an act wherein God winked at sin and passed by it in simple kindness. Wrote Luther,

> Were this view true, the entire New Testament would really be vain and futile, and Christ would have labored foolishly and uselessly in suffering for sin. God Himself would have practiced jugglery and humbug without any need, because He might well have forgiven and not imputed sins without the suffering of Christ. . . . Although out of pure grace God does not impute our sins to us, He nonetheless did not want to do this until complete and ample satisfaction of His law and His righteousness had been made. . . . God ordained for us, in our stead, One who took upon Himself all the punishment which we had deserved and fulfilled the Law for us; thus He averted the judgment of God from us and appeased His wrath. Grace . . . was purchased with an uncalculable, an infinite treasure: the Son of God Himself. Therefore, it is . . . impossible to obtain grace except through Him alone.[1]

As the apostle John wrote, "grace and truth came through Jesus Christ" (John 1:17). Paul set this truth before us when he said that we are justified not only by His grace but also "by His blood" (Romans 5:9 NASB).

One of the major points to be made about Christ's life and death as the sole basis for our salvation is that this view takes seriously the law and justice of God. No one can be justified unless the law is perfectly fulfilled. The death of Christ upholds the inviolability of the law. It magnifies God's justice fully. The law must be kept for us to be *justly* saved. And Christ kept the law fully and paid for all its demands on behalf of those who violate it. He redeems those who by grace put their faith in Himself.

It is here that the dangerous tendency to antinomianism ("against the law") is properly checked in the experience of true believers. We have come to Christ alone. In Him we are redeemed, and by Him we are kept by the Holy Spirit in grace. Faith will not turn to sin as a way of life because Christ *has* become our life.

If our salvation is accomplished entirely by the mediation of Christ in human history, then His perfect life and substitutionary atoning death alone are able to save us. When faith becomes secularized the person of Christ becomes increasingly associated with the popular whims of the culture. In such an environment a substitution of wholeness for holiness takes place. And feelings are substituted for informed and vital faith. What is needed is to put Christ back in the center of our vision so that He is genuinely preeminent in our lives.

Faith Alone

Even though justification and reconciliation are solely by grace alone and through Christ alone, not all sinners are justified and redeemed. Only those who take the warnings of the Savior seriously and look to Him will be saved.

Luther stated this well when he wrote, "Although the work of redemption itself has been accomplished, it still cannot help and benefit a man unless he believes it and experiences its saving power in his heart."[2] There are two very important things we must note about the faith that brings the believing sinner to grace.

First, faith is not magic. There is no saving virtue in faith as faith. Faith does not make one right with God; it merely receives the gift that makes one right with God. It does not bring grace into existence; it becomes conscious (by the Holy Spirit) of something already there. It is, as one person put it, like opening your eyes to see the sun that was always there before you ever saw it. Opening your eyes does not make the sun shine. Believing does not magically make you a Christian.

Second, faith is not an attribute of the natural human heart. Rather, it is a gift God gives to us. He gives this gift to us through the preaching of the gospel and by the work of the Holy Spirit. This is what the apostle Paul had in mind when he wrote to the Ephesian congregation, saying, "It is by grace you have been saved, through faith—and this is not from yourselves, it is the gift of God—not by works, so that no one can boast" (Ephesians 2:8-9).

We must understand what faith is if we are to grasp this fundamental principle. Faith, biblically, is a noun that corresponds to the verb that means "to believe." Faith is the biblical term consistently used to explain the relationship into which the gospel calls people—a covenantal relationship of trust in God through Christ. Faith involves right belief about God. Thus, orthodoxy is a fundamental part of true faith (see Galatians 1:8-9; 2 Thessalonians 2:13; Titus 1:1; and 1 Peter 1:22), but it is more than orthodoxy, for it brings us, by the Spirit, into living and abiding in Christ as our personal Savior.

Faith, furthermore, rests on divine testimony. Writes theologian James I. Packer, "The Bible views faith's convictions as certainties and equates them with knowledge (1 John 3:2; 5:18-20), not because they spring from supposedly self-authenticating mystical experience, but because they rest on the testimony of a God who 'cannot lie' (Titus 1:2) and is therefore utterly trustworthy."[3] But faith that truly rests upon Christ alone, and the grace of God alone, is a supernatural gift. Sin and Satan have blinded us. We cannot "see" unless God gives us light (John 3:3; 1 Corinthians 2:14; 2 Corinthians 4:4; Ephesians 4:18), and we cannot "come" to trust Christ until the Holy Spirit has worked within us, giving us both the sight and the desire and will to come.

This must be stated very plainly: *Faith does not save.* A host of present-day evangelicals carelessly, or perhaps foolishly, misunderstand this point when they say, "You will be saved by faith!" It is vital that we state this as Paul says it: "For it is by grace you have been saved, through faith—and this not from yourselves, it is the gift of God" (Ephesians 2:8). Please note the prepositions carefully: "by" grace and "through" faith.

Faith is resting, trusting, cleaving, and hoping. It is taking God's promises for what they actually are. In regard to justification it is taking God's declaration at face value: "To the man who does not work but trusts God who justifies the wicked, his faith is credited as righteousness" (Romans 4:5). Present faith in Christ secures present "eternal life" in full fellowship with God the Father through Christ alone (John 5:24; 17:3).

Many in our time do not understand or faithfully embrace this great truth. We have allowed sociological methods of church growth to undermine this essential truth. The sharp distinction between the church's true biblical Word has been blurred by a marketing orientation that seeks to make the gospel more and more appealing to more and more people. In doing this we have denied the foolishness, or the offense, of the cross (see 1 Corinthians 1:18). We have also lost the power of the message in the process (see 2 Corinthians 2:1-5).

We must understand afresh that there is no gospel without the imputation of Christ's righteousness to those who believe. Because He is the basis for our acceptance before God, patriotism, good works, and moral decency are not to be associated with the ministry of the gospel of Christ. Both evangelicals and Catholics alike need to understand that a commitment to moral reformation is not the same as a commitment to the gospel of a crucified Redeemer.

This doctrine of justification through faith alone is an offense. It troubles the proud. It directly challenges the "good, clean, righteous" person who supports the church faithfully. It offends the person who considers his experience of God to be adequate for salvation. It bothers the victorious people who often speak of their ecstasies of the Spirit and visions of the supernatural. But to all who have struggled mightily with God's law and His holy character and have seen their own unrighteousness, this is the only hope they have—a merciful, good, gracious God giving to them solely on the basis of faith. This is based on the righteousness of Christ alone by grace alone. Hallelujah, what a Savior!

Scripture Alone

The assurance that God had spoken in the past and that He still speaks through the Scriptures gave the Reformers incredible boldness in standing up to the grave errors they saw in the medieval church. As Luther said near the end of his life, in reference to the Reformation, "The Word did it all!"

The constant battle cry of the Reformation was, "Scripture alone!" This truth formed the whole cause of the Reformation. It sustained the recovery, and it drove forward every entrance of divine light that brought revival. It will do the same in your life and that of your church fellowship if the same principle is truly recovered today.

What was it that made this principle so powerful, and what exactly is meant by "Scripture alone"? The Roman Catholic Church had believed, even on the eve of the Reformation, in an infallible Bible. It accepted the same texts as the Reformers, at least until the Council of Trent, when the apocryphal books were formally recognized. What was new about the "Scripture alone" position of the Reformers?

The new element the Reformers brought to the church of their age was the conviction that Scripture can and does interpret itself to the faithful from within itself—Scripture is its own interpreter. The Christian does not need popes or councils to explain what Scripture really means. Scripture has a self-authenticating authority. Further, Scripture actually stands over papal and conciliar pronouncements, showing them to be untrue when they go against the written Word. Scripture was *both the only source and the only judge* of what the church had said and should say in any age. If we want to speak with the Lord's authority, we must speak according to the Scriptures!

By the sixteenth century the authority of Scripture had been weakened in a number of ways. One way was that human traditions were exalted, and another way was that the truths of Scripture were communicated to the common people through the mediation of popes, councils, and priests. The Reformers, in stating the great principle "Scripture alone!" were setting forth the idea that God speaks to His people directly, finally, effectively, and authoritatively through His written Word.

This vital message is needed today more than ever. Whether the Catholic reader recognizes it or not, there still is singular power in the truth of Scripture. Until recently many Catholics never seriously read their Bibles. With the freedom of Vatican II "opening the window," this, thankfully, has changed in the last 30 years. Now Catholics attend Bible study groups with both fellow Catholics and evangelicals. They are finding out for themselves what I mean when I speak about Scripture's power to grip the heart *directly* when the Bible is read in faith. One does not need a human agent to see the glory of Christ revealed on the sacred pages of God's Word. One only needs the gift of God's Spirit, who is our Teacher (John 14:26), for which all should pray when they come to the infallible Scripture.

Too many evangelicals do not truly trust Scripture, either. In increasing numbers they are turning to what their favorite teacher says or to a popular bestselling book. For them Scripture has been separated from its authoritative function. It has become a marketing text, or even a book to be used in developing therapeutic techniques. They do not carefully search the Scriptures as the Bereans (Acts 17:11) of the New Testament era. Some evangelicals even add their own special set of cultural and religious rules and rituals, including a list that is tailored to each special area of the country.

Many evangelical pastors neglect Scripture's primary place in their instruction by introducing one fad after another into their ministry. They adapt the message of the Bible to fit the "felt needs" of their hearers (consumers) or even allow precious doctrinal truths to lose their salient force for good by emptying the true authority of the Bible in the way that they handle it week by week. What we all need is a great recovery of faith found by looking to Scripture alone.

There is much talk in our time about the ministry of the Holy Spirit, among both Catholics and evangelicals. Indeed, this talk and emphasis has done much to bring us together. But we must understand afresh that the work of the Holy Spirit in personal experience can never be separated from the written Scriptures. The Spirit does not speak clearly except through the Word of God. Apart from the written Word we would never know or understand the grace of God. This is the test of truth, period!

But did the sixteenth-century Reformers understand the Bible to be their *only* authority? Absolutely not! They appealed to history, science, logic, church fathers, councils, creeds, confessions, and careful studies of the Greek and Hebrew texts. But what they did say was that there is only one ultimate, final authority—the Bible alone.

When the early church convened its first council to decide upon matters that threatened its own unity, the appeal was not to human authority. Its appeal was not to Rome, to one of the apostles, or to some higher human court. The appeal in Acts 15 was to "the words of the prophets," which are said to "agree" regarding God's acceptance of the Gentiles into the visible church on the same ground of grace as the Jews (verses 12-18).

Thirty-three times the writers of the New Testament say, "As it is written. . . ." A most important example is to be found in regard to the doctrine of justification by faith alone in Romans 1:17, where we read, "In the gospel a righteousness from God is revealed, a righteousness that is by faith from first to last; just *as it is written*: 'The righteous will live by faith.'" Here Paul grounds his entire doctrine of justification by faith in the words of the prophet Habakkuk. Don't miss this point: Faith alone, in other words, is grounded in Scripture alone. Paul appeals to the authority of Scripture repeatedly in Romans (see, for example, 4:3; 10:11).

A particularly common phrase that indicates the same principle is found in Luke 24:44-47, where we read of Christ being written about "in the Law of Moses, the Prophets and the Psalms" (verse 44). When Jesus began to teach His disciples about all that He was and all that He had done for their redemption, He "opened their minds so they could understand the Scriptures" (verse 45). And in verse 46 He said to them, "This is what is written...." If you read the New Testament looking for an appeal by Jesus or the apostles to tradition, creeds, councils, or church authority, you will look in vain. In fact, such an appeal is condemned several times in the Scriptures (see Isaiah 29:13; Matthew 15:1-9; and Colossians 2:8).

In the sixteenth century, the practice of exalting human traditions to a place above the Word of God had weakened the authority of the Scriptures. The same problem exists in a myriad of ways in the modern church, Catholic and Protestant. The formative principle of the Reformation movement, and a major difference that still remains between Catholics and evangelicals today, is Scripture alone. This is true because the Scriptures—and the Scriptures only—speak directly, authoritatively, and powerfully to the people of God. That is why, whether you are Catholic or Protestant, Christian or non-Christian, the Spirit of God speaks powerfully to your life when you read the Word of God in faith, study it carefully in your home Bible study group, or hear it preached effectively.

A famous minister of the last century, when asked if he should defend the Bible, said, "Defend the Bible? Why, it is a lion! I would rather let it out. It can defend itself!" Scripture alone still says today, "Let the lion out! It is true authority, and it will be the instrument the Holy Spirit uses to bring people to the knowledge of true faith and holy practice."

Summing Up

Historian J. H. Merle d'Aubigne wrote many years ago, "The only true reformation is that which emanates from the Word of God." Ultimately the greatest fruit of the evangelical recovery of the sixteenth century may very well be lost if we continue to turn away from the gospel and the Word of God.

Many important concerns face modern Christians. Our culture is collapsing. Values we hold dear in Western civilization are eroding. Secular intellectual barbarians are scaling our city's walls. Multitudes of concerned people are wringing their hands. Leaders are continually calling upon us to stem the tide. "Get involved," they urge us. "Do something if you really care. Join hands with the forces that oppose immorality and secular humanism in our society." At times it seems that Christianity has been turned into a massive coalition of uniquely nontheological ministries all aimed at "doing something" to rescue us before it is too late.

My greatest fear is not that we will lose Western culture, or even our great nation. My greatest fear is that we will lose the gospel. Evangelicals were given this great truth but they have no singular claim to it. This message is for all who will receive it, Catholic or evangelical. If we lose the gospel, the result will be a fallen church. We will have no real power. And we will have nothing with which to truly change the culture, one significant person at a time.

Most people today no longer understand the doctrine of Scripture alone; thus frequent attacks upon this precious truth no longer alarm us. Evangelicals undermine the doctrine of faith alone when we ignore the centrality of this truth and its importance. We do this as well when we enter into agreements that turn away from this distinctive truth. We do this when we continually build ministries on something other than Christ alone and grace alone.

Catholics do this too when they read their Bibles and then turn back to the Catholic mystery to settle the vital issues of repentance and faith. It is just too easy to solve the problems of the heart with answers received from human authorities. We all have this tendency; only God can break us of it.

But the answer is not far from any of us—evangelicals need to be evangelical again! And Catholics need to truly submit themselves to the magisterium of holy Scripture. Until we all recover our biblical heritage, turn to the Word of God afresh, and plead for His mercy to fall upon us, we will continue groping for a center of reference. We are like a weakened and powerless Samson, going round and round in circles without our eyes.

A few rays of hope are emerging as increasing numbers of Christians become aware of what the Reformation was *really* about. Many are beginning to see the significant doctrinal reasons for what actually took place. They are daring to dream of another reformation in our present-day generation. They are praying earnestly for a reformation that draws from the past yet looks to the future with hope. May God be pleased to light another blaze in the church that transforms our culture with amazing effect. And may He light that blaze in both evangelical and Catholic hearts.

A Personal Invitation

This book has been written with two kinds of readers in mind. First, the evangelical who still believes that the Scriptures really are the infallible Word of the living God. To this reader I conclude by asking you to "do your best to present yourself to God as one approved" (2 Timothy 2:15) in every way possible. I urge you to grow in the grace and knowledge of the Lord Jesus Christ. You have a doctrinal and personal heritage in your faith and practice that you may know very little about. Learn more about it.

Seek to understand more what you believe and why you believe it. Keep a watchful eye on the events of our time that threaten to undermine the Reformation truths of sound evangelical religion. If you do not know what you believe and why you believe it, you will not be equipped for every good work, and you will be easily led astray.

It is my belief that evangelicalism is in trouble in the present age. Not because we are not large, nor because we are not active or vocal, but rather because we do not understand what it means to be truly evangelical. The tragic consequences of our weaknesses are becoming more apparent every day.

This book has also been written for Roman Catholic readers who wish to better understand the beliefs and practices of contemporary (that is, Vatican II) Roman Catholicism. My appeal to you is also personal.

Have you trusted Jesus Christ alone to save you from sin—both its enslaving power and its fatal consequences? Do you really know that if you died today God would accept you into His heaven? On what basis? If your answer in any way reveals that your hope is in the Catholic mystery (i.e., your hope is grounded in your baptism, your fellowship with the church, or the faith and intercession of others), you will not be saved. You must trust Christ and Him only.

Further, do you understand that unless you are saved by grace alone you cannot and will not be saved at all? God does not save you because of your human will or personal decision. He does not save you because you are a "good Catholic" (or a "good evangelical," for that matter). He will save you solely on the basis of His grace, or you will not be saved.

Do you see that you have sinned? Few Catholics I have met deny this truth. Actually, Catholics sometimes understand this reality much better than evangelicals. But have you personally felt the weight of your sin? Has the law of God brought you to see your helpless, hopeless, and powerless condition before Him? If so, cast yourself upon His mercy and ask Him to save you.

Finally, do you understand that if grace comes to you in any way other than by faith alone, then you are sharing in the work of salvation? God will not share this work with you. Either He must save you based upon His free gift, or you will not be saved. If you contribute anything, even your faithful receiving of grace through the partaking of sacraments, then you are not trusting Him alone.

Ultimately you must obey the Word of God as the Holy Spirit speaks to your conscience. For this to happen you must know the teaching of the Scriptures. You must search the

Scriptures earnestly that you may find the truth. You may well discover that there are far more conflicts between the plain teaching of the Word of God and your Catholic tradition than you ever imagined. We have seen only a few of these in this book.

If you follow the Word of God it may cost you dearly. Jesus Himself taught:

> Do not suppose that I have come to bring peace to the earth. I did not come to bring peace, but a sword. For I have come to turn "a man against his father, a daughter against her mother, a daughter-in-law against her mother-in-law—a man's enemies will be the members of his own household." Anyone who loves his father or mother more than me is not worthy of me; anyone who loves his son or daughter more than me is not worthy of me; and anyone who does not take his cross and follow me is not worthy of me. Whoever finds his life will lose it, and whoever loses his life for my sake will find it (Matthew 10:34-39).

But if you follow God, faithfully obeying His Word, you have everything to gain and ultimately nothing to lose, for Jesus also said, "Whoever acknowledges [or confesses] me before men, I will also acknowledge [confess] him before my Father in heaven" (verse 32).

Notes

Chapter 1—The Holy Catholic Church

1. Philip Schaff and J. J. Herzog, *The New Schaff-Herzog Encyclopedia of Religious Knowledge* (Grand Rapids, MI: Baker, 1977), 4:222.
2. Mark A. Noll, *Turning Points: Decisive Moments in the History of Christianity* (Grand Rapids, MI: Baker, 1997), pp. 66-67.
3. Charles Colson and Richard John Neuhaus, eds., *Evangelicals and Catholiocs Together* (Dallas: Word, 1995) p. 104.
4. Ibid., pp. 104-5.

Chapter 2—The Dark Ages?

1. Mark A. Noll, *Turning Points: Decisive Moments in the History of Christianity* (Grand Rapids, MI: Baker, 1997), p. 122.
2. Mary Clark, ed., *An Aquinas Reader* (Garden City, NY: Doubleday, 1972), p. 481.
3. Noll, *Turning Points*, pp. 122-23.
4. John Armstrong, *Roman Catholicism: Evangelical Protestants Analyze What Divides and Unites Us* (Chicago: Moody, 1994), p. 45.

5. Ibid., p. 48.
6. Ibid., p. 50.
7. Ibid., p. 56.
8. Hans J. Hillerbrand, ed., *The Oxford Encyclopedia of the Reformation* (New York: Oxford Press, 1996), II: 314-15.

Chapter 3—The Great Evangelical Recovery

1. John Armstrong, *Roman Catholicism: Evangelical Protestants Analyze What Divides and Unites Us* (Chicago: Moody, 1994), p. 65.
2. Ibid., p. 253.

Chapter 4—A Fallen Church?

1. Ibid., p. 256.

Chapter 5—The Central Mystery of the Christian Faith?

1. Scott Hahn, *Rome Sweet Rome: Our Journey to Catholicism* (San Francisco: Ignatius, 1993), p. 88.
2. Ibid., p. 89.
3. *A Catechism of Christian Doctrine*, rev. ed. (London: Catholic Truth Society, 1985), p. 47.
4. Joseph Cardinal Ratzinger, ed., *Catechism of the Catholic Church* (New York: Catholic Book Publishing Co., 1994), p. 334.
5. Ibid.
6. Pope Pius XII, *Mediator Del*, no. 68.
7. Karl Keating, *What Catholics Really Believe: Setting the Record Straight* (Ann Arbor, MI: Servant, 1992), p. 53.
8. Ibid., p. 66.
9. Ratzinger, *Catechism of the Catholic Church*, pp. 351, 354.

10. Paul Johnson, *The History of Christianity* (London: Weidenfeld & Nicholson, 1976), p. 99.
11. Ibid., pp. 101-2.
12. Robert Godfrey in John Armstrong, *Roman Catholicism: Evangelical Protestants Analyze What Divides and Unites Us* (Chicago: Moody, 1994), p. 73.

Chapter 6—Seven Sacraments?

1. Joseph Cardinal Ratzinger, ed., *Catechism of the Catholic Church* (New York: Catholic Book Publishing Co., 1994), pp. 289-90.
2. Ibid., p. 289.
3. Ibid., p. 292.
4. Ibid., p. 322.
5. Ibid.
6. Ibid., p. 292.
7. Peter M. Stravinskas, *Catholic Encyclopedia* (Huntingdon, IN: Our Sunday Visitor, 1991), p. 369.

Chapter 7—Who Really Speaks for God?

1. Peter M. Stravinskas, *Catholic Encyclopedia* (Huntingdon, IN: Our Sunday Visitor, 1991), p. 707.
2. Ibid., p. 761.
3. D. A. Carson, "Matthew" in *Expositor's Bible Commentary*, vol. 8, Frank Gaebelein, ed. (Grand Rapids, MI: Zondervan, 1986), p. 368.
4. Ibid.
5. Ibid., pp. 368-69.
6. Joseph Cardinal Ratzinger, ed., *Catechism of the Catholic Church* (New York: Catholic Book Publishing Co., 1994), pp. 233-34.
7. Vatican Council I, "The First Dogmatic Constitution on the Church of Christ," session 4, chapter 4.

8. Ibid.
9. Vatican Council II, "Dogmatic Constitution on the Church," no. 25.
10. Vatican Council II, *De Ecclesia,* p. 22.
11. Ibid., p. 25.
12. Stravinskas, *Catholic Encyclopedia*, p. 939.
13. Ibid.
14. Ibid., p. 615.
15. Donald MacLeod in Sinclair B. Ferguson, David F. Wright and James I. Packer, eds., *New Dictionary of Theology* (Downers Grove, IL: InterVarsity Press, 1988), p. 143.

Chapter 8—Spiritual Life and Devotion

1. Peter M. Stravinskas, *Catholic Encyclopedia* (Huntingdon, IN: Our Sunday Visitor, 1991), p. 901.
2. John Armstrong, *Roman Catholicism: Evangelical Protestants Analyze What Divides and Unites Us* (Chicago: Moody, 1994), p. 143.
3. See John H. Armstrong, ed., *The Compromised Church* (Wheaton, IL: Crossway, 1998).
4. Ibid., p. 155.
5. Stravinskas, *Catholic Encyclopedia*, p. 848.
6. Ibid.
7. A. A. Lambing, *Sacramentals of the Catholic Church* (New York: Benzinger Bros., 1892), pp. 151, 173.
8. Stravinskas, *Catholic Encyclopedia*, p. 607.
9. Vatican Council II, *De Ecclesia,* p. 8.
10. Paul G. Schrotenboer, *Roman Catholicism: A Contemporary Evangelical Perspective* (Grand Rapids, MI: Baker, 1989), p. 32.
11. See Joseph A. Fitzmyer, *The Gospel According to Luke* (Garden City, NY: Doubleday, 1981), and Raymond E. Brown, *The Birth of the Messiah* (Garden City, NY: Doubleday/Anchor, 1993).

12. Pope John Paul II, *Redemptor Hominis* (Boston, MA: The Daughters of St. Paul, n.d.), pp. 56-57.
13. Stravinskas, *Catholic Encyclopedia*, p. 860.
14. "What's in a Vision?" *U.S. News & World Report*, March 12, 1990, p. 67.
15. Ibid., pp. 67-69.
16. "The Case of the Weeping Madonna," *U.S. News & World Report*, March 29, 1993, pp. 46-51.
17. "What's in a Vision?" p. 69.

Chapter 9—Death and the Life to Come

1. Thomas Bokenkotter, *Essential Catholicism: Dynamics of Faith and Belief* (New York: Doubleday, 1986), p. 241.
2. Ibid., p. 242.
3. Ibid., pp. 242-43.
4. Ibid., p. 245.
5. H. M. Carson, *Roman Catholicism Today* (Grand Rapids, MI: Eerdmans, 1964), p. 110.
6. Joseph Cardinal Ratzinger, ed., *Catechism of the Catholic Church* (New York: Catholic Book Publishing Co., 1994), p. 266.
7. Ibid., pp. 268-69.
8. Ibid., p. 275.
9. William J. Cogan, *A Catechism for Adults* (Youngstown, OH: Cogan Productions, 1975), p. 50.

Chapter 10—The Present Hour

1. John Armstrong, *Roman Catholicism: Evangelical Protestants Analyze What Divides and Unites Us* (Chicago: Moody, 1994), p. 84.
2. George Weigel, "Post Vatican II," *Eternity*, October 1986, p. 21.
3. Peter M. Stravinskas, *Catholic Encyclopedia* (Huntingdon, IN: Our Sunday Visitor, 1991), p. 955.

4. Armstrong, *Roman Catholicism*, p. 187.
5. Pope John Paul II, *Crossing the Threshold of Hope* (New York: Knopf, 1994), p. 149.
6. Ibid., p. 139.
7. Joseph Cardinal Ratzinger, ed., *Catechism of the Catholic Church* (New York: Catholic Book Publishing Co., 1994), p. 218.

Chapter 11—Is Evangelical Really Enough?

1. Charles Colson, "Evangelicals and Catholics Together: The Christian Mission in the Third Millennium," *Institute on Religion and Public Life*, November 14, 1994, p. 136.
2. John Armstrong, *Roman Catholicism: Evangelical Protestants Analyze What Divides and Unites Us* (Chicago: Moody, 1994), p. 284.
3. Boniface Ramsey in John Armstrong, *Roman Catholicism,* p. 285.
4. Ibid.
5. John D. Woodbridge, "Why Did Thomas Howard Become a Roman Catholic?" *Christianity Today*, May 17, 1985, p. 48.
6. Ibid., p. 57.
7. Howard Thomas, *Evangelical Is Not Enough* (San Francisco: Ignatius, 1984).
8. Scott Hahn, *Rome Sweet Home: Our Journey to Catholicism* (San Francisco: Ignatius, 1993).

Chapter 12—Recovering Biblical Christianity

1. Ewald M. Plass, ed., *What Luther Says: A Practical-in-Home Anthology for the Active Christian* (St. Louis: Concordia, 1987), 2:709.
2. Ibid., 2:706.
3. James I. Packer in Everett F. Harrison, ed., *Baker's Dictionary of Theology* (Grand Rapids, MI: Baker, 1985), p. 209.

For Further Reading

For those who wish to study more about Catholicism and evangelical Christianity there are several books that make for useful resource material.

For those who are beginners I would suggest the following evangelical treatments:

Schrotenboer, Paul G., ed. *Roman Catholicism: A Contemporary Evangelical Perspective.* Grand Rapids, MI: Baker, 1989.

> This small book (99 pages), which is the result of a study done by members of the World Evangelical Fellowship Theology Commission, carries a lot of informed and useful interaction with contemporary Catholicism.

Webster, William. *Salvation: The Bible and Roman Catholicism.* Carlisle, PA: Banner of Truth, 1990.

> The author, a former Catholic, has done extensive research, understands his subject well, and writes lucidly. Highly recommended.

Coffey, Tony. *Once a Catholic.* Eugene, OR: Harvest House, 1993.

This was written by an Irish evangelical minister who left Roman Catholicism and maintains a genuine love for his former fellowship and its people.

McCarthy, James G. *The Gospel According to Rome: Comparing Catholic Tradition and the Word of God.* Eugene, OR: Harvest House, 1995.

McCarthy, another former Catholic, writes well, deals with real doctrinal differences, and uses his sources very accurately.

White, James R. *The Roman Catholic Controversy*. Minneapolis: Bethany House, 1996.

White handles the evangelical *solas* of the Reformation well and applies them to contemporary Catholicism accurately. He is a writer who can take important theological truths and make them accessible.

Regarding Roman Catholic resources for beginners, I would recommend the following:

Ratzinger, Joseph Cardinal, ed. *Catechism of the Catholic Church*. New York: Catholic Book Publishing Co., 1994.

Not so much an old question-and-answer catechism in simple form but rather a systematic treatment of post-Vatican II theology, both belief and practice. The definitive source for the study of the current teaching of the magisterium and Pope John Paul II.

Bokenkotter, Thomas. *Essential Catholicism: Dynamics of Faith and Belief*. New York: Doubleday, 1986.

A very readable and easy-to-handle book that explains and defends Catholic belief succinctly.

Keating, Karl. *What Catholics Really Believe: Setting the Record Straight*. Ann Arbor, MI: Servant, 1992.

Accomplishes well the author's stated purpose—clarifying mistaken notions about Catholic belief and practice commonly held by both Catholics and Protestants.

For more academic study of Roman Catholicism written by evangelical authors, I would recommend the following:

Armstrong, John H., ed. *Roman Catholicism: Evangelical Protestants Analyze What Divides and Unites Us.* Chicago: Moody, 1994.

A conciliatory treatment that takes seriously post-Vatican II changes but strives to explain and defend Reformation theology.

Althaus, Paul. *The Theology of Martin Luther.* Philadelphia: Fortress, 1966.

An important work that will help the serious student understand how Luther's theological insights shaped the Protestant response to Roman Catholic doctrines.

For more academic study of Roman Catholicism written by Catholic scholars I would recommend the following:

Hastings, Adrian, ed. *Modern Catholicism: Vatican II and After.* New York: Oxford University Press, 1991.

An authoritative one-volume guide to the Catholic Church and its development over the past 25 years. A must for serious readers who want to understand Catholic thought and life today.

Ratzinger, Joseph Cardinal. *Principles of Catholic Theology: Building Stones for a Fundamental Theology.* San Francisco: Ignatius, 1982.

The leading contemporary defender of the magisterium's doctrine provides a must book for modern reflection.

Note

The reader should understand that this is a short list of resources and that the author endorses none of them in their entirety but merely recommends them as learning resources.

Answers to quiz at the end of chapter 4 on page 68.

1. a
2. a
3. a
4. b
5. a
6. b
7. b
8. a
9. a
10. a

Other Good Harvest House Reading

WHEN GOD MOVES

by John Armstrong

Many Christians today are genuinely seeking revival. Many claim to be experiencing true revival as God "awakens" them, insisting that the accompanying "holy laughter" and unusual behaviors are truly the work of the Holy Spirit. Other believers are wary, pointing out excesses and seeming contradictions with Scripture.

THE GOSPEL ACCORDING TO ROME

by Jim McCarthy

Drawing directly from the new *Catechism of the Catholic Church*, the author addresses the primary differences between Catholic doctrine and biblical Christianity. A clear, accurate comparison of Catholic tradition and the Word of God.

WHY THE CORSS CAN DO WHAT POLITICS CAN'T

by Erwin Lutzer

Many Christians assume the only way to save America from moral collapse is through involvement in politics and social reform, but pastor and bestselling author Erwin Lutzer points out the real battle in America is spiritual, not political.